EAT SMART
EAT RAW

KATE MAGIC

This book is dedicated to everyone who has bought one of my books, come to an event, or eaten some of my food over the past ten years. I am blessed to be at the heart of a movement of people dedicated to self-love, personal transformation, and making the world a more beautiful place for everyone. Thank you. We are just beginning.

Originally published in 2002
This new edition published in 2013 by Grub Street
4 Rainham Close, London SW11 6SS
www.grubstreet.co.uk

A CIP catalogue for this book is available from the British Library
ISBN 978-1-909166-06-6

Printed and bound by MPG Printgroup Ltd
Grub Street uses FSC (Forest Stewardship Council) paper

Contents

Introduction

MY STORY

I first embarked on a raw food diet in September 1993. I had found myself instinctively wanting to eat a lot of fruit and salads, and had heard from friends how health-giving an all-raw diet could be. As the kitchen of the house I was staying in was out of action for three months while it was being renovated, I decided to try it for myself. I took the plunge, and lived on fruit all day, with a big salad and Essene bread and tahini for dinner (neither Essene bread nor tahini are strictly raw, but I didn't know that then). By the time the kitchen was back in order, I was hooked on my new diet, and have stuck with it ever since. Of course, I have had my ups and downs – it is a huge challenge to stick to 100% raw, 100% of the time. Raw fooders often talk in percentages, claiming to be '70% raw' or '90% raw' but just to achieve 50% long term can make a vast difference in your life.

Although I was convinced of the health benefits, and had experienced for myself how much better I felt, at first the idea that I would stop eating cooked foods altogether was too much, and I would binge on biscuits and crisps. But gradually, I came to recognise that eating these foods didn't make me feel as good as when I made my raw food choices. However much I would think that I loved a cooked treat, even one as harmless as apple crumble, when I indulged I would be disappointed, as the cooked dishes came to taste lifeless and dull to me. My body was adjusting to the new levels of energy and the sense of liberation that raw foods gave me, and cooked foods left me on a downer. I began to realise that of course I *could* eat whatever I wanted – but what I really wanted was to feel good all the time. The cleaner my system, the more cooked foods left me with a 'hangover'; feeling sluggish and irritable. Gradually, the redundancy of cooking food became a reality to me, and the desire to eat it slipped away completely. Anyone who has become a vegetarian, given up smoking, or overcome any addiction in his or her lives, will understand that feeling of a part of your daily life becoming an anathema.

As a teenager I had experienced a very rocky relationship with food. Some people say that raw food diets encourage or even create eating disorders; for me it was the reverse, as discovering raw foods helped me to overcome my problems with food. Since adolescence I had been trapped in a binge-fast cycle, where I would fast for days, and then overeat to compensate. I believe this was due in part to my instinctive recognition that the foods I was eating weren't right for me: I would reject them, only to be eventually overcome by hunger and greed, which would then be followed by repulsion at all the rubbish I had put into my body. Raw foods were a revelation: at last I could eat as much as I wanted, and not feel terrible. Eating half a dozen biscuits made me feel sick and tired; eating half a dozen apples left me feeling overfull, but not ill. Over time, as my body got used to being fed, nurtured and respected, the desire to overeat slipped away. As food no longer disturbed my internal balance, my fear of it disappeared.

Now I am astounded at how little I need to eat. I rarely feel ravenously hungry, and feel satiated after relatively small portions of food. Because on the raw diet all our foods are nutrient-dense, the body's requirements are met quickly and efficiently. This in turn means that the body needs less energy for digestion, fighting toxins and excreting poisons, so it is much less demanding in its requirements. If you want to lose weight then stop counting calories and start counting nutrients! Over-eating happens when the body is searching for nutrients – the brain is waiting for the signal to say that the body has what it needs, and it never comes, so you keep ploughing your way through that packet of biscuits, unconsciously looking for the vitamins and minerals you will not find there. In addition, I used to find it very difficult to wake up in the mornings, and needed eight or ten hours of sleep a night otherwise I felt terrible. Now, because my body is working more efficiently, I don't wake up feeling fuzzy, but fresh, alert, and ready to go, and average just six hours a night.

When I adopted the raw food diet, I found, in common with many others, changes happening on all levels of my life. Primarily, I experienced a great leap in energy levels: my body was no longer expending such huge amounts of energy on digestion, and so I felt an immediate improvement in my vitality. Also quickly apparent was a greater mental clarity and focus. I felt sharper, more alert, and after a long time on the diet I am really conscious of having the resources to be constantly on the go without flagging. Along with these more obvious changes, I also became aware of changes on a deeper level; I am now much happier and lighter, as the positive energy of raw foods fills my being. I am less prone to bad moods and depression, and more satisfied and content. I have a greater tolerance of difficult people and situations, but at the same time know better where my boundaries lie, and what I am prepared to put up with. I notice things in nature that I never did before: the trees look more green and alive, and the changing of the seasons is more apparent to me. All these elements combine to increase my zest for living hugely, leading to a more positive and productive lifestyle. Because I am eating food that is pure and undamaged, I feel whole – more at one with myself and the world around me.

Over the years, I've experienced all the different angles on being raw. At the start, I jumped straight in at the deep end, 100% raw, including a two-week apple fast just before Christmas. Then Christmas came, and I went 100% cooked! After a few months I stabilised at about 50%, then gradually built it up over the next few years until I was 100% again by 1995. In 1996 I did nine months on fruit only, which was amazing at first, but difficult to sustain. At the end of that year, I found out I was pregnant and it was back down to 50% again, gradually building back up to 90%. I stayed there for a while, only eating cooked foods on social occasions when I felt it would be too impolite to refuse. Once I'd been raw about ten years, I noticed all cooked cravings had disappeared, and for the past decade I have been fully raw. I don't like to say 100%, because I'm sure I must eat some things unintentionally sometimes, such as raisins which have been heat-treated, and I also consume some superfoods, herbs and seasonings which are not raw. But the last time I sat down to a cooked meal must be well over ten years ago. I can say hand on heart that I feel amazing, and every year it just gets better. Every year my levels of vitality grow, and I experience more and more bliss bubbling through my cells. It's remarkable to be feeling that my life is still beginning and everything is opening up before me, and though I wouldn't claim to be reversing the ageing process, I definitely seem to be holding back the years.

Many leading raw foodists advocate 100% raw as the only way to go, but I believe this is too difficult for most people. Undoubtedly, the benefits of being 100% are huge, but we live in a world where we are constantly coming into contact with cooked foods, and to refuse them continually is both challenging and awkward. Holistic health is as much about having a healthy mind as a healthy body, and the constant denial of other foods can be more harmful than the foods themselves. If you can maintain just 50% raw, you will experience a huge increase in your wellbeing. Try eating a side serving of raw food with every meal at first, then when you have got used to this, gradually increase the size of the raw portion to the cooked portion, until you have reached a level that you feel comfortable with (many people find this is around 70%). There are so many borderline foods: nuts, dried fruits, olives, seasonings, and dehydrated goodies, that are not strictly raw, making it difficult to be completely sure about what you are eating. Ultimately, so long as you are eating a diet of fresh, organic wholefoods, with fruit and vegetables as the main elements in your diet, you can't go far wrong. One word of warning, however: it is not uncommon for raw foodists to have trouble with their teeth. Fruit acids destroy the tooth enamel and cause decay. Fresh fruit is not as damaging, but the concentrated sugars in dried fruits and juices can cause problems. If you are worried about your teeth, avoid 'grazing' (snacking throughout the day) and practice good dental hygiene. Make sure you are including plenty of calcium in your diet, and check how you are getting your vitamin D, which is a hard to find nutrient on the raw vegan diet.

Naturally, most of us are unable to incorporate such huge changes into our lifestyle overnight. On a physical level it isn't hard to do, but food carries deep emotional resonance, and for most of us it is these ties that are difficult to break. Initially, we can be faced by feelings of alienation from our peers, and the sense of missing out on things. But, through perseverance, these feelings fade, and we are left with a vitality and youthfulness that more than make up for anything we may be missing. I still go to restaurants frequently; I usually phone the day before, and state my requirement for a raw vegan salad as my main course. Friends and family may be suspicious at first, but when they see how well you are doing, they usualy take on board some of the philosophy themselves. When I eat at other people's houses, it's much easier for them to prepare some fresh fruit and vegetables, than to cater for any other way of eating; it's equally easy for me to bring a dish myself. If you approach the diet with a positive attitude, others will too; if they see you being guarded and awkward, they are more likely to start interrogating you. If the subject comes up in general conversation, I just say that I am a vegan. If they ask what I do, I say I teach healthy eating. If people are genuinely interested, then I love to talk about raw foods, but I have learnt from experience that if people are not ready to entertain the concept, it is best left alone altogether.

I believe that raw fooders will become more and more accepted over the next few years, to the same degree that vegetarians are now. When I was a child, vegetarianism was still highly unusual and regarded as cranky. Now, every restaurant and café has a vegetarian dish, and people are prepared to accept the fact that it is possible, even preferable, to live without meat on a daily basis. I hope that by the time my children are adults, raw foods will be equally integrated into our culture, and people will see the logic of eating food that has not been killed by the cooking process, just as they can now see the logic of not eating an animal which has been killed.

WHY EAT RAW FOODS?

Raw foods have a long and venerable history, dating right back to Biblical times. In *The Essene Gospel of Peace*, a reputedly overlooked book of the Bible, Jesus advocates eating raw foods.

> 'But I do say to you Kill: neither men nor beasts, nor yet the food which goes into your mouth. For if you eat living food, the same will quicken you, but if you kill your food, the dead food will kill you also. For life comes only from life, and from death comes always death. For everything which kills your foods, kills your bodies also. And everything which kills your bodies kills your souls also. And your bodies become what your foods are, even as your spirits, likewise, become what your thoughts are. Therefore eat not anything which fire, or frost, or water has destroyed, Fire burned, frozen and rotten foods will burn, freeze and rot your body also.'

The raw food movement as we know it today really grew out of America in the early 90s. Raw food isn't a new concept by any means; I believe historically, we would have always eaten a lot of raw foods, just because it's easier and more convenient than cooking. Eating organic foods now is seen as a luxury, but until about 60 years ago, eating local, seasonal and organic was the only option most people had! In the same way, our early ancestors would not have bothered to build a fire every time they wanted to eat. But recent interest in the benefits of raw food started with people like Anne Wigmore and Viktoras Kulvinskas in the 80s. David Wolfe and Gabriel Cousens are two of the big names who popularised this way of eating among health-conscious Americans in the 90s, and their ideas spread across the water to Europe.

In the UK, the Fresh network was founded by Susie Miller in 1992 and was the beginnings of the current movement over here. I was an early member, and actually edited the newsletter for a few years around the millennium. Our company Raw Living was founded in 2002, when this book first came out. Originally we sold only a handful of products; now we stock hundreds of products and ship all over Europe every day. The raw food movement has really gathered pace in Europe in the past five years, and now there are many online stores, cafés, restaurants, and teachers all over the continent, with more starting up all the time. It's a very exciting time to be getting into raw foods, as it is such a vibrant community, and there is so much support and information to draw on. For a long time, the Americans were really leading the way: there were many more books, chefs, educators, restaurants, and convenience products available there than in Europe, where there was virtually none. Now I feel Europe is catching up very quickly, and it's a huge blessing to meet and work with all these people who have so much energy, passion and joy in what they do.

I would just say, that as it is a movement that is still in its infancy, it's important to validate the information you receive yourself. As yet there is no raw certification like there is organic certification, so if you are not sure, always question suppliers as to the temperatures their products have been heated at. There are a lot of products labelled as raw which actually aren't, if you dig a little deeper. Equally, if you're listening to teachers, ask what their experience and background is; I do believe no-one can fully grasp raw foods and the effects the diet has on the body, until they've been doing it at least ten years, and while they might be able to inspire you to find out more about raw yourself, it's unlikely they will have a full understanding of what the diet is really about. There are a few raw accreditation courses in Europe and the USA (I teach courses myself), but many enthusiastic people set themselves up as chefs or educators when they don't necessarily have the experience and knowledge such a role demands.

If you are a left-brain dominant person who likes logical and rational explanations, with everything scientifically proven, I'm afraid you are going to be disappointed with the scant research that there is about why raw foods are so beneficial. It's worth pointing out here, that the pharmaceutical industry is actually the richest industry in the world, with a higher profit than any other sector, way above even banking and arms. There is a huge amount of money tied up in the business of sickness, and subsequently it is very difficult to share information that will help people take their health back into their own hands and liberate them. We sell many products that have been used for hundreds and even thousands of years in their countries of origin, with wonderful reputations for healing specific diseases and keeping the body strong and healthy, yet we are not allowed by law to state what these might be on our website or our packaging because the products have not been tested in a Western scientific laboratory.

What little research we have dates back to the first half of the 20th century, before the pharmaceutical industry really got a stranglehold. I would love to have more evidence at my disposal to back up my testimonial and the thousands of testimonials I have heard from other people as to the efficacy of a raw food diet, but the research simply isn't there. I think as we understand more about how to create true health, a lot more evidence will come to light, but for now it's a diet you have to experience to believe. I believe it's a further testament to its efficacy that so many people choose to explore it and then stick with it, when there is so little understanding of why it really works.

In 1930, Swiss physician Dr. Paul Kautchakoff showed that eating cooked food causes leucocytosis, that is, an increase in white blood cells. Effectively, the body recognises cooked food as a poison, and reacts accordingly, as it would with any poison entering the system. Cooked food is treated as a foreign body, so an immune response occurs; this does not happen when raw foods are eaten. Thus eating cooked foods regularly puts a strain on the immune system that eating raw foods does not, explaining why raw foodists tend to have more energy and be less susceptible to illness. Furthermore, the body cannot just distinguish raw food from cooked, but it recognises how denatured the food is, and produces more leucocytes accordingly. For example, the body reacts more strongly to white flour than to whole-wheat flour, and junk foods such as hot dogs cause a reaction akin to food poisoning. Cooked foods can be eaten without causing leucocytosis if they are eaten with raw foods, and raw foods make up more than half of the meal. This is a great point to understand while you are transitioning. As long as your meal is at least 50% raw, and you eat the raw foods first or with the cooked foods, you will still get many of the benefits of the raw diet. But at the same time, you can still enjoy all your favourite cooked foods, and don't have to struggle with cravings or social issues.

Another experiment in 1946 by Dr. Frances Pottenger, conducted on 900 cats, showed the degenerative effects of cooked foods. He divided the cats into three groups: one group was fed raw meat and unpasteurised milk, the second group received only cooked meat and pasteurised milk, and the third group was the control group, who got half and half. Over a ten-year period, the cats fed on raw foods thrived, while those on the cooked diet became progressively dysfunctional. Each generation of 'cooked-food kittens' had poorer health and died younger, until Pottenger actually had to stop the experiment because there weren't enough of the 'cooked-food' cats to carry on; they were literally dying out. This is tragic, but I believe we can correlate what happened there with what's happening in our society now. We are seeing the highest levels of all kinds of diseases from heart disease to cancer, diabetes, obesity, autism, and ADHD. As I already mentioned, it's only in the past few generations that a diet not composed of whole foods has been possible, not alone common. It seems obvious to me that our current levels of chronic illness are directly related to the gradual decline in the quality of our diets over the past half a century.

From an ecological perspective, raw food is an incredible relief to the planet's resources, and a potential solution to world hunger. Raw food requires little or no packaging, and no processing, saving energy and emissions. No cooking also conserves energy, and saves money on fuels (dehydrators are economical to run). Finally, all the waste is compostable and biodegradable, so we are not adding to the burden of rubbish that must be disposed of. Then there is the convenience aspect – although some of the recipes need time to prepare, it is possible to knock up a gourmet raw dinner in just a few minutes, and as for fruit, it is surely the ultimate convenience food. Furthermore, the NHS would save unimaginable amounts of money in not having to treat so many illnesses: there are thousands of people around who have used raw foods to successfully treat diseases such as cancer, heart disease, diabetes, and skin and gut disorders. The Hippocrates Health Institute was founded in Boston, USA in 1970 by Dr. Ann

Wigmore, and has a long record of successfully treating people with life-threatening illnesses. Of course, diet alone cannot heal the body, but it can go a long way in supporting the body in healing, in conjunction with other therapies, whether conventional or holistic.

When we cook our foods, we lose a lot of the nutrients. Vitamin C and all the B group vitamins are heat-sensitive, and are considerably diminished by cooking. But it's the enzymes that make the real difference, and where the real magic of raw food lies. Enzymes are a much neglected part of nutrition, but just as vital to health as vitamins and minerals. They are present in every living thing, and can be likened to the lifeforce, the prana or the chi of the animal or plant. We need them for every function in the body, life cannot happen without them. They are completely destroyed by heat; the general consensus is that food heated over 42°C (108°F) no longer contains any enzymes. When we are children our bodies create enzymes all the time, but when we enter adolescence we stop manufacturing them. By this point we have built up a large store, but they gradually get used up by life's processes. If we do not replace them with the enzymes found in live foods, or with enzyme supplementation, our reserves get depleted, we age more quickly, and it gets harder for the body to maintain good health. The more enzymes we have in our diets, the more we look and feel young, which explains raw fooders' general youthful appearance and vitality.

I am not exaggerating at all when I say that I feel younger every year. If you look at photos of me from five or ten years ago, I definitely look younger now than I did then. Every year, I understand my body better, and so am better equipped to respond to its needs. I have so much energy and enthusiasm for life; my mind always feels clear, I am always happy, I don't remember the last time I was sick and I need very little sleep. I have never been this fit and healthy in my life. Every year gets better, and I see no reason why that won't continue for decades to come. It's an incredible feeling that we don't really have words for. I can't accurately represent this sense of abundance, empowerment, liberation, and endless possibility and potential that comes from really listening to your body and being at one with its needs. It's a deepening relationship that, like any relationship, becomes more fulfilling over time, and with the more I put into it. Take your first steps on this path, and you will begin to get an inkling of what I am talking about! No matter where you are in your life, including more raw foods in your diet is going to make you feel happier, stronger and more energised.

SO WHAT DO YOU EAT?

If you start researching the raw food diet, you may become a little confused. There are so many different approaches to the diet and a lot of people keen to tell you that you have to eat this or mustn't eat that. You have the 80/10/10 school of thought which advises eating mostly fruits, with small amounts of fat and protein. My understanding is that this is not a balanced diet and is actually dangerously unhealthy in our northern European climate. Then you have Hippocrates, who say no fruit at all, but lots of sprouts and juices. Their regime is very effective, but impossibly strict to sustain in normal everyday life. And you've got people like David Wolfe, who advocate consuming a ton of expensive superfoods with long and unpronounceable names; I am also a big fan of superfoods, but think it's more important to address the basics of the diet first, and just use superfoods as the cherry on the cake, if you like, not as a substitute for a balanced diet.

I think it's interesting that actually nearly everyone I know who has been doing the raw food diet in this northern European climate for any length of time, comes to the same conclusions as to what works best. My experience is that what gives us the most sustained energy levels and strong immune system is a low-glycaemic, relatively high fat diet, based around local seasonal organic vegetables. I also believe that unfortunately, however well we eat, we cannot get all we need from our food. We lead fast-paced, pressured lives that take their toll on the body. We have to contend with huge amounts of environmental pollution inside and outside the home, that our grandparents and their ancestors did not have to put up with. More importantly, due to intensive agriculture policies, the soil is depleted and even organic produce does not contain the same levels of vitamins and minerals that it used to. To ensure the favourable health of my family, we add to our diet superfoods such as Klamath Lake blue-green algae, bee pollen and maca on a daily basis. None of these are supplements – all are foods in their own right – superfoods, in fact. I would class a plant as a superfood if it has an exceptionally dense nutritional profile, as well as having energetic properties that means it also heals on a spiritual and emotional level, like flower essences or homeopathy. As well as doing a great deal to ensure long term health and increased immunity, they boost energy levels considerably.

My understanding is that there are three principles that are essential for the good health of the body. These are being properly hydrated, being in an alkaline state, and having an abundance of healthy fats in the diet.

A lot of people are scared of consuming fats and oils, but healthy fats form the building blocks of the cells and are an essential nutrient. When we eat plenty of these fats, our bodies recognise that there is no need to store them, and so we convert them into fuel. In fact, fats are the main source of fuel on the raw food diet, and especially important in the cold winter months. There are three types of fat we need: saturated fats, which we can find in coconuts and cacao; monounsaturated fats which we find in olives and avocados; and the polyunsaturated fats that are found in seeds. Out of the seeds, hemp, flax and chia are especially necessary as they are the only vegan dietary sources of the essential fatty acids, omega 3, 6, and 9. I recommend trying to consume one or the other of hemp, flax or chia every day on any kind of vegetarian diet.

I am an avid believer in drinking large quantities of water. Some raw foodists say that water is unnecessary with the diet, but I have always seen it as a food in its own right. Water is an element necessary for life, and the body cannot function efficiently without it. I consume a large amount of fluid every day including juices, teas, and superfood milks. We commonly misinterpret thirst as hunger, and eat when in fact we are simply in need of liquid nourishment. Try gradually increasing the amount of liquid in your diet, and you will quite literally feel your body becoming more fluid. However, it is best not to drink with meals, as liquids weaken the digestive juices; drink half an hour before meals, or at least two hours afterwards.

Our diets need to be composed mainly of alkaline foods. Acidity in the body causes stress and stress causes acidity. In the West, we have a tendency to get locked into acidic cycles. The most common responders to stress are alcohol, tobacco, sugar and caffeine, all of which are highly acidic! Grains, pulses, dairy products and meat are also acidic. The best way to alkalise is to consume large amounts of greens and vegetable juices. The two top foods for alkalising are barley grass and wheatgrass.

Most health-conscious people are aware of the principles of food combining. Basically stated, this involves not mixing different classes of foods, such as proteins and starches, to aid digestion and absorption. These rules still apply when eating raw foods, but on a high raw diet you can be more relaxed about them, as the high enzyme content of the foods helps considerably with digestion. But don't go overboard, for instance by trying to create a traditional three course dinner, and including lots of nuts, sprouted grains, vegetables and fruits all in the same meal. Many people who are new to the diet experience problems with abdominal discomfort, bloating and flatulence because their digestive systems, which have been weakened by decades of cooked food eating, cannot cope with the powerful action of raw foods. This is one reason why it is best to introduce raw foods gradually, and to consider a course of colonics to help restore digestive health (see page 14). When eating raw foods, the main rule to remember about food combining is to eat fruits separately, and not mix them with other food groups.

I do not recommend the consumption of animal products of any kind. If you do feel that meat, fish and dairy products are something you don't want to give up, then do your best to source organic foods from farms where the animals have been humanely treated. Few people advocate the consumption of raw meat; it can cause all sorts of digestive problems, including parasites. However, there are a significant number of raw fooders who include raw dairy products in their diets. Dairy products are a good source of vitamin D, which is hard to find on a vegan diet, so this is something you may want to consider. Unpasteurised dairy products are not as mucus-forming as pasteurised dairy products. I don't believe meat and dairy products are unhealthy per se, but it is modern farming methods, the way the foods are processed, and the amounts they are consumed in which make them problematic to the body.

The foods that people find hardest to give up are wheat, rice, soya, corn and potatoes. Bear that in mind and don't struggle with your cravings! Instead make sure to enjoy everything you choose and eat it without guilt. Have a big salad with it and minimise the damaging effects on your body. It was ten years before I honestly felt I didn't care if I never ate potatoes again! Be patient with yourself.

Wheat contains a natural opiate, and many people are addicted to bread because of its sedative effect. Unfortunately, wheat has been intensively farmed for too long now, and many people are finding they can no longer tolerate it. If I think back to my childhood, we often ate wheat at every meal: cereal for breakfast, sandwiches for lunch, pasta or pie for dinner, as well as wheat-based snacks in the form of crisps, cakes and biscuits; it is no wonder my body has had enough and rejects it if I try to eat it now. People think of whole-wheat organic bread as a healthy food, but consider how the wheat grain got to the plate: it was harvested, milled, made into bread, cooked, packaged, and then sent to the shops – how much life force can be left in it by then? Far better to buy wheat grain and sprout it – most people who cannot tolerate wheat can eat it sprouted because of the enzymes released in the sprouting process, which turn the starches into more easily digestible sugars.

It is best to avoid large quantities of soya, which contains an oestrogen-mimicking chemical, and stresses the pancreas. Potatoes also cause great stress to the body, as they are so high in sugar. Rice cakes are thought of as healthy, but there is evidence to suggest that the puffed grains may be toxic. Rice is also acidic in the body. If you have an overwhelming craving for a food that you know isn't going to do you any favours, don't ignore it. The best way to deal with it is to prepare yourself a large green salad, and eat that first, or as an accompaniment. By filling up on the salad, you will be less likely to overeat on your treat, minimise its negative effects in your body, and maybe even reduce the craving for it.

Although nuts form an essential part of a raw food diet, they should be eaten in small quantities only, and carefully prepared. When nuts are cooked, the fats in them become indigestible. All commercial nut butters are made from heated nuts; the best raw brand that I know of in the UK is the Sun and Seed brand. Nuts that we buy in the shops are more often than not heat-treated to preserve them, even when bought in their shells. Cashews, macadamias and pine nuts are never raw, unless you buy them from a dedicated raw food company such as Raw Living. The only way to be sure about other nuts is to directly check with the supplier; Infinity, for example, have started labelling whether their nuts are heat-treated or not. Peanuts are the worst nuts of all and should be avoided completely – highly indigestible and potentially carcinogenic (according to an FDA report), even organic ones – likewise pistachios, which contain a toxic fungus under their shells. All shelled nuts should be soaked before you use them, for 4-8 hours, to release the enzyme inhibitors and make them more digestible. Sometimes it is acceptable to grind them to a fine powder before use, so they are already broken down and more easily utilised by the body. Seeds are much easier on the system than nuts, and should be soaked for 2-4 hours. Dried fruits are usually heat-treated, and for that reason shouldn't be eaten in large quantities. Olives are another food that usually aren't raw – try to buy fresh from a deli rather than in a jar or tinned, or one of the specific raw brands such as Olives et Al and Raw Health in the UK.

In summer, raw food eating comes naturally and instinctively, but winter may seem more of a challenge. This is when cravings for cooked comfort foods are more likely to hit us hard. In reality, once you adjust to this way of eating, winter is no more difficult than any other time of year. In fact, you are less likely to feel the cold: when you eat hot food, your body has to work harder at regulating its internal temperature whereas when all your food is eaten at room temperature, it is easier for your body to retain its warmth. Many raw foodists find they revert to that childlike state of not feeling the cold at all. However, bear in mind that it is unhealthy to eat cold food all year round. One of the most common misconceptions about raw food is that it has to be cold. Forty two degrees C is actually quite warm – think hot tubs! So enjoy gently heated soups and stews, and burgers and sauces warmed in the dehydrator. Drink lots of herbal teas, and make extensive use of thermogenic spices such as chilli, garlic, ginger, and cinnamon. I find myself eating more concentrated foods such as dehydrated crackers and seeds. In the summer, I gravitate towards more salads and juices.

Often raw food literature will make claims that children instinctively love raw foods over cooked foods. In my experience this is not true! I believe that their tastes are formed in the womb, so what you eat when you are pregnant is crucial to forming their preferences once they are born. However, pregnancy is not a time to be changing your diet or going on any kind of a detox, so if you are in a position to, I recommend you do your cleansing work before conception in order to give your child the best start in life. This doesn't mean that we cannot educate our childrens' palates, just that it's harder work. My main techniques were bartering – 'if you eat a banana you can have some soya dessert', or 'eat some more cucumber and I'll give you another rice cake'; and plain sneakiness, for example, blending raw veggies like celery and carrots into a pasta sauce (see page 50) or putting maca and flax oil into a yoghurt. All three of my boys eat a mostly raw diet, and that is what they ask for because that is all we have around the house. But on social occasions I never make a big deal out of it, and let them eat whatever vegan food is on offer, so they do not feel too restricted. I always carry snacks, and if we are going somewhere where I know there will be foods they don't eat, I will bring their own treats with me. If you are trying to add raw food to your children's diets, I cannot overemphasise the importance of striking a balance. A disturbing number of children in the West overeat on junk foods and suffer from malnourishment and constant illnesses. If you can encourage your children to eat just a little raw food a day, you are setting them up in beneficial habits for life. But don't worry if they are reluctant – don't starve them in an attempt to push the diet on to them! Making sure they have a balanced diet based around whole foods is far more important than whether they eat raw or not. And consider the benefits of a supplement such as Klamath Lake blue-green algae or maca, that you can add to their drinks or favourite snacks, which will act as a safety net and ensure they are getting a dose of all the nutrients they need. I go into much more detail on feeding children in my book *Raw Living*.

Finally, remember that raw foods alone cannot make us healthy. Exercise is essential and should form an integral part of your life. Yoga, walking, cycling, swimming and rebounding are all excellent forms of exercise that are easy to incorporate into your daily routine. Rebounding is similar to trampolining and can be performed while you watch TV, or in a snatched five minutes between appointments. At the same time, make sure that you include adequate rest and relaxation. Too many of us nowadays are constantly on the go, don't get enough sleep, and so don't allow the body time to recover and restore energy naturally. Adrenal fatigue is commonplace, especially in cities. No matter how well we eat, if we don't give the body time for renewal, we become depleted and run down. Furthermore, research repeatedly shows that our mental state has a more profound effect on our health than our diet. Keep a positive outlook, a balanced, non-judgmental attitude to life, and seek to develop the self in all things. The point of doing this diet is to feel good. Always bring it back to that – it's about loving your body and having a good relationship with it, not forcing it to eat things that make it uncomfortable.

Colonic hydrotherapy is a useful treatment, especially when you are embarking on a raw food diet. If your stomach is at all rotund, if you experience a lot of gas, if you are tired immediately after eating: you are likely to have impacted matter in the colon, which is often years old, and rots and decays, preventing efficient food absorption. You can have the best diet in the world, but if you aren't absorbing the food efficiently, it will do you no good. Have a course of colonics initially to clear you out, and then continue with them at regular intervals. I also recommend regular home enemas, which aren't as deep cleansing as colonics, but can be easily and inexpensively administered in the comfort of your own bathroom. I personally usually have at least four colonics a year, and do a home enema at least once a month.

If you do fall ill, homeopathy and acupuncture are both excellent forms of treatment. Many people choose to make regular monthly visits to a holistic practitioner as a form of preventative medicine, to support their systems and keep everything in balance. This is known as constitutional treatment, which builds up and strengthens the whole person, but can also be used for acute conditions when necessary. Find a reputable homeopath or acupuncturist who can get to know you and your family, and will know the right remedies to prescribe when you need them.

I consider an alkaline diet that is high in raw foods, and includes superfoods and plenty of liquids and healthy fats, as well as daily exercise, sun and fresh air, adequate rest and relaxation, positive outlook, regular naturopathic cleansing, and a sound relationship with a homeopath, acupuncturist, or other holistic therapist, the fundamental precepts of well-being. My understanding is that if everyone made these simple lifestyle changes, levels of disease would drop dramatically as we all obtained superior levels of health. Furthermore, these measures are all inexpensive to implement, and our economy would benefit from a fitter workforce, and huge savings for the health service. When we look after ourselves like this, we are so much less likely to fall sick, and when we do come down with something, our bodies have the strength and resources to fight disease off quickly and efficiently, without too many unpleasant symptoms.

I sincerely hope that you are inspired and empowered by this book. It has come out of over two decades of my experience of eating raw, and finding foods that my family, friends and I enjoy, as well as being easy and simple to prepare in our ever-busy lives. Most people I speak to who are interested in their health, know that eating raw is beneficial, but don't know where to begin in adding raw foods to their diet. With little or no experience of gourmet raw cuisine, it is hard to move beyond the idea of raw foods being just salads and fruit. My wish is that this book opens a doorway into a cuisine and lifestyle which is fun and exciting, and in doing so brings you closer to your true unlimited potential, granting you the energy and enthusiasm to live a wonderful, joyous, fulfilling and rewarding life that continually surpasses your expectations and leads you along the path of bliss, magic and miracles.

Practicalities
EQUIPMENT

A JUICER

Juicers are easy to find now, and you can buy one for as little as £20 on the high street. However, wouldn't recommend the cheaper models as they aren't very efficient, and you need a lot of fruit to make a decent amount of juice. At the other end of the scale the most popular models such as the Green Power sell for upwards of £300. Nowadays, I recommend that people use their blender to make juice, and then strain it through a milk bag (see opposite). This way, you get maximum juice with minimum effort and wastage, and it's one less piece of expensive equipment to worry about.

A DEHYDRATOR

If you are serious about eating more raw foods, I recommend a dehydrator as an essential purchase (available in the UK from Raw Living). A dehydrator is a simple box with a fan, a heating element and trays for the food inside. It warms food at a very low temperature: effectively cooking it without killing it, so technically it is still raw. Because it uses minimal heat, it takes a very long time to dry things out – anything up to 24 hours. I have an Excalibur 9-tray, which I use two or three times a week, and would find it very challenging to feed my family without it. If you're finding it difficult to give up bread and biscuits, this is the way forward – for raw cookies and crackers they are incomparable. They're equally indispensable for using up leftover produce – just slice it up, dry it out and you've got some great snacks. If you do not have a dehydrator, you can use a conventional oven and have it on the lowest heat possible, with the door ajar – this should heat the food at around the same temperature. Fan ovens work best, and Agas work as well. You could leave dishes that need dehydrating for shorter periods, such as burgers, in a warm place, for instance an airing cupboard (although this would not work for biscuits and breads which need more drying). If you moved to another country, you could dry produce out in the sun too, but we never get enough sustained hot temperatures in this country to make that possible. In California, I met a man who had built his own solar powered dehydrator. Dehydrated goods keep indefinitely if stored in an airtight container, in the fridge if possible.

RECOMMENDED FRUITS – pineapple, pear, banana

RECOMMENDED VEGETABLES – tomatoes, peppers, onions, greens

Or you can blend leftovers together, spread the mix on the trays, and make fruit and vegetable leathers. I make fruit leathers out of bananas and whatever other fruits I've got lying around at the end of the week.

FOOD PROCESSOR/BLENDER

For serious mixing, you want a high power blender. There are many different makes on the market now; I use the Omni-blend and a Thermomix. They perform virtually every food preparation task you can imagine with great speed and efficiency. High power blenders break down the cells in the food, increasing bioavailability, so the body is able to absorb more nutrients. The Thermomix is wonderful because you can use it as a set of scales, and you can also heat food in it. This aspect is surprisingly useful for raw fooders because you can set the temperature at 37°C and gently heat your food knowing it's still raw. Other popular makes of high power blender are the Vitamix and the Blendtec.

If these pieces of equipment are out of your price range, ideally you need a food processor with a mixer bowl, a blender, and a grinder attachment. Sometimes called a spice mill, this little attachment is essential for grinding nuts and seeds.

A lot of the recipes in this book call for the use of a high power blender or a food processor. Basically, a high power blender will do more or less everything a food processor will do, but a food processor cannot do everything a high power blender can do.

YOU ALSO NEED

A really good, sharp KNIFE (I recommend a ceramic knife).

A pair of small SCISSORS for chopping herbs and dried fruits.

Some tablespoons, measuring cups and scales for MEASURING (I use measuring cups more than scales).

A BEATER for making salad dressings by hand.

A cook's THERMOMETER for testing the temperature when gently heating dishes.

A MILK BAG, as previously mentioned, for making milks and juices. This is a muslin bag that acts as a strainer for liquids. It comes with a drawstring handle so you can hang it up from your kitchen cupboards. Can also be used for sprouting, raw cheese making, and as a travel sieve. Machine washable and very durable.

A SPIRALIZER for making raw noodles and spaghetti. Spiralizers have at least two different settings, so you can make noodles or ribbons. Most commonly used with courgettes and carrots, but you will find that all root vegetables work well. Easy and fun to use.

SPROUTING

You can buy many different kinds of sprouters that are very efficient at raising sprouts, but I just use large jars or bowls that I keep next to the sink. Larger sprouts can just be rinsed once a day in the morning, but the smaller ones need to be done twice a day, especially in hot weather. There are many others to experiment with, but below is a list of the ones that I use the most. I always have some alfalfa on the go, and at least a couple of others. In hot weather, things sprout quicker, which is why you will find that sprouting times given in most American books aren't long enough for our colder climate. All nuts should be soaked for at least a few hours prior to use. This activates an enzyme, which make them more easily digestible.

Put whatever it is you are sprouting in a large (1 litre) jar, add approximately double the volume of water, and leave to soak for the stated time. People have a tendency to over soak their sprouts; if they start to rot and fail to sprout properly, this is usually the reason why. When you have finished soaking, rinse, and drain and leave to sprout, rinsing just once a day. Once your sprouts are ready, keep them in the fridge and eat them within a few days. Quantities given make approximately one jarful.

ALFALFA 1 tbsp, soak 2-3 hours, sprout 5-7 days. Alfalfa is an easy sprout to raise, and a staple of the raw food kitchen.

BUCKWHEAT 150 g/5 oz, soak 4-5 hours, sprout 2-3 days. Buckwheat needs careful attention to stop it turning slimy. Rinse it well before and after soaking and be careful not to over rinse.

CHICK PEA 60-90 g/2-3 oz, soak 6-8 hours, sprout 3-4 days.

LENTIL 90 g/3 oz, soak 5-6 hours, sprout 3-4 days.

MUNG BEAN 45 g/1½ oz, soak 5-6 hours, sprout 3-4 days.

OAT GROATS 125 g/4 oz, soak 4-6 hours. Does not sprout – use within a day or two.

QUINOA 150 g/5 oz, soak 3-4 hours, sprout 2-3 days. Quinoa needs careful rinsing before sprouting, or it will go off. Don't over soak, and rinse twice a day.

SUNFLOWER SEEDS 125 g/4 oz, soak 2-4 hours, sprout 2-3 days. Another staple that is straightforward to sprout.

WHEAT GRAIN 45 g/1½ oz, soak 6-8 hours, sprout 3-4 days. Wheat grain must be eaten within a day or two, or it starts to grow green, indigestible shoots (which if left become wheatgrass). You can also try rye, spelt and kamut as alternatives to wheat.

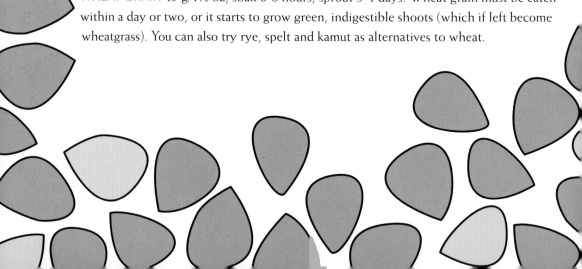

SHOPPING

If you care about your food at all, you will already be eating organic. Organic food is the best option for so many reasons: not least, it is the only real alternative if we want to preserve our wonderful English countryside, help restore the soil quality and encourage wildlife. The vitamin, mineral, and enzyme count in organic produce can be as much as 50% higher than in non-organic produce, and by consuming organic foods, we avoid exposing ourselves to poisonous chemicals and potential carcinogens.

Since I began eating raw foods, the taste difference between organic and non-organic has become glaringly obvious; the flavours of organic food are far superior. At first sight organic food may seem more expensive, but it is worth paying the extra to get the better quality and nutritive value. Furthermore, what many people do not realise are the hidden costs of non-organic farming that we pay for with our taxes: the subsidies that only non-organic farmers get, and the huge costs of cleaning up the damage done to the environment by agro-chemicals.

Most supermarkets are now well stocked organically. In the UK I think Waitrose is by far the best for range and quality of items, and ethics of sourcing and production. But if possible, I believe it is better to avoid supermarkets, and support your local, independent shops. As people are becoming increasingly aware, the bigger corporations are less easy to hold accountable and more likely to manipulate the market. Ask your greengrocer if he can stock the most popular organic lines; most are happy to oblige, and can often undercut the supermarkets by a great deal. Health food stores are always keen to advise on items, are generally more knowledgeable than supermarket staff, and often have better quality produce. In recent years there has been a proliferation of box schemes and farmers' markets. In a box scheme, you pay a weekly fee to have a selection of fresh organic fruit and vegetables delivered to your door. Farmers' markets are set up to allow you to buy direct from the producer. Wherever you shop, try and buy locally grown, seasonal produce whenever possible – not only does it contribute to the economy of this country, but it will be much tastier and fresher than something which has travelled miles to get here, causing unnecessary pollution on the way.

If you are serious about adopting this way of eating, you would do well to start purchasing ingredients in bulk. Items such as nuts and dried fruits can be expensive, but if you buy 5 kg at a time, the price is reduced drastically, by as much as 50%. These items keep well, so there is no need to worry about over-stocking, and as well as saving money, you cut down on packaging. Search online for a health food co-operative such as Suma or Infinity; there will be a minimum order value, but it's usually not difficult to reach, especially if you team up with some like-minded friends. Otherwise your health food store should be willing to order items in for you.

Raw Living sells all the hard to find raw grocery items and superfoods, as well as a wide range of raw snack products such as crackers, crisps and chocolates. There are quite a few raw food stores online now, in Europe and the USA.

WHAT TO BUY

FRUIT

Buy organic and locally grown produce, in season wherever possible.

Staples: apples, bananas, oranges, pears, grapes, lemons, limes, grapefruits, dates, and all kinds of berries.

Plus there are a whole host of exotic fruits to discover, including mango, papaya, guava, lychee, mangosteen, rambutan, plantain, kumquats, dragon fruit, star fruit, jack fruit, and the king of fruits, durian. These should be eaten minimally, unless you are visiting the countries in which they are grown and are able to eat them fresh.

VEGETABLES

Again, for superior quality, buy organic, locally grown, in season produce.

Many vegetables can be difficult to digest raw, so blend them into soup, or grate them and marinade them overnight.

Staples: broccoli, cabbage, carrots, onions, avocados, spinach, lettuce, celery, cucumber, tomatoes, peppers (not green ones, they are unripe and hard on the digestion), mushrooms, beetroot, courgettes, radishes, corn, green beans, olives, cauliflower.

There is a wide variety of leafy greens which should start to form an important part of your diet, such as kale, pak choi, cavalo nero, Chinese leaf, rocket, lambs leaf, watercress, chicory, mizuna and purslane. Green leafy vegetables are one of the most nutritious food groups. Or try some of the more unusual vegetables such as mooli, jerusalem artichoke, celeriac, fennel or kohlrabi.

People neglect the root vegetables such as parsnips and squash, but they can be eaten raw if grated and marinated or blended into a soup.

SEA VEGETABLES

Dulse, arame, hijiki, nori (flakes and sheets), kelp and kelp noodles, sea spaghetti, wakame.

An essential part of anyone's diet. They contain more minerals than any other kind of food, as well as many vital vitamins. For example, dulse contains fifteen times more calcium than cow's milk.

Seagreens is the brand name for wild wrack granules which I also use a lot.

HERBS AND SPICES

Essential for turning a plain dish into something special.

Fresh: ginger, garlic, red chilli, parsley, and as many other fresh herbs as you can afford, or preferably, grow.

Dried: cinnamon, cumin, garam masala, Chinese five spice, paprika, nutmeg, cloves, cayenne, coriander, turmeric. I am particularly fond of the Turkish spice known as sumac.

NUTS

Walnuts, almonds, cashews, coconut (brown), brazils, hazelnuts, pecans, pine nuts, macadamias.

I use coconut flakes a lot; not all brands are raw.

Nut butters, e.g. almond, walnut.

SEEDS

Sesame, sunflower, pumpkin, hemp, flax, alfalfa (for sprouting only), chia.

Seed butters, e.g. tahini, hemp butter, pumpkin butter.

Hemp comes as the whole seed which are grey and quite bitter, and as shelled seed which is white, sweeter, more flavoursome and more versatile.

When I mention activated nuts and seeds in a recipe, these have been soaked, sprouted, marinated and dehydrated, making them flavoursome, crunchy and super healthy. You can do this yourself if you have a dehydrator (page 16) or buy the pre-packaged variety.

DRIED FRUIT

Avoid fruits that have been sulphured, such as light apricots and pears.

Raisins (preferable to sultanas), apricots, figs, prunes.

Dates – try and buy fresh rather than dried wherever possible. If I haven't specified, it means either is acceptable for the recipe but I recommend fresh over dried because they will be raw and have a higher nutritional value.

Goji berries are Chinese berries that are packed with nutrition, including tons of protein and B vitamins.

Mulberries come from Iran and have a gorgeous chewy texture and honey flavour.

GRAINS

Wheat, oats, quinoa, buckwheat, spelt, rye.

No oats found in health food stores are raw, not even the oat groats. We have raw oats at Raw Living that we get straight from the farmer.

BEANS AND PULSES

Lentil, chick pea, mung bean, aduki.

OILS

Flax and hemp oils are raw, but cold pressed oils aren't, necessarily. Extra virgin olive oil is raw.

Flax, hemp, extra virgin olive oil, coconut.

SWEETENERS

There is no perfect raw sweetener. Try not to depend on any one too heavily.

AGAVE SYRUP a lot of agave brands around aren't raw. It's a good low glycaemic sweetener, and as it's very sweet you only need to use in small amounts.

RAW HONEY buy honey from a small independent producer, it's an entirely different product from supermarket, mass-produced honey. Not strictly vegan.

YACON SYRUP yacon comes from a South American vegetable and is suitable for diabetics and those on an anti-Candida diet as the sugars in it are not absorbable by the body.

XYLITOL made from fermented birch bark, makes a great sugar substitute. It has a low GI and is actually good for the teeth, hence its inclusion in chewing gum.

COCONUT SUGAR not raw, but high in minerals and low glycaemic index.

CAROB, LUCUMA, MESQUITE these are low glycaemic powders used in raw cakes and sweets. Carob and mesquite are pods, lucuma is a fruit.

STEVIA only made legal in the EU in 2012, stevia is a highly concentrated sweetener which is also suitable for diabetics or people on anti-Candida diets.

FERMENTED FOODS

Look out for ones that are unpasteurised, these should be raw.

Sauerkraut is the most well-known but look for kimchi, which is a Korean ferment, or fermented vegetables like beetroot and carrot. You can make your own quite easily. I buy the Cultured Probiotics brand from Raw Living, which I love.

FLAVOURINGS

NUTRITIONAL YEAST FLAKES add a cheesy taste to foods, high in B vitamins and minerals, not raw.

MISO get unpasteurised. Although not strictly a raw food, because of the enzymatic activity, it is a living food.

TAMARI or SHOYU tamari has a more intense flavour, shoyu is slightly mellower. Tamari is wheat-free. Whenever I have specified tamari in a recipe, shoyu can be substituted if you prefer.

LIQUID AMINOS a raw version of soy sauce. In the UK, the Marigold brand is most widely available.

APPLE CIDER VINEGAR unpasteurised vinegar is raw. Look for vinegar containing the mother, which is the natural ferment. I use other vinegars such as balsamic and rice vinegar but they are not raw.

SUN-DRIED TOMATOES may not actually be sun-dried! I buy them in packets, then marinate them myself. Or you can dehydrate fresh tomatoes yourself.

VANILLA use vanilla powder, or buy fresh pods and grind them.

LIVE SOYA YOGURT containing beneficial probiotics. If you're not vegan, you can use raw unpasteurised goats' and sheeps' yoghurt if you can find it.

LECITHIN GRANULES are derived from soya or sunflower. Lecithin is an emulsifier, so it is useful for thickening recipes. It also contains an important brain nutrient called phosphatidyl choline which is only otherwise found in eggs. If you are a vegan who is not eating eggs regularly it's important to include a lecithin supplement in your diet.

SALT I use any kind of natural rock salt. Himalayan crystal salt is very popular. Rock salt contains minerals and actually helps us absorb more minerals from our food. I love Herbamare as well which is a mix of herbs and salt.

NUTRIENTS

I haven't trained in nutrition, and this is by no means an exhaustive list, but a summary of where the most important nutrients for health can be found in a raw food diet.

PROTEIN

Mother's milk contains only 2% protein, and babies do a massive amount of growing fed on this alone. This would indicate that we don't need as much protein in the diet as we are led to believe.

Sources: all nuts and seeds, especially walnuts, pumpkin seeds and sunflower seeds. Sprouts, especially, buckwheat, quinoa, and wheat. Soya, miso.

FATS

Many people avoid fats for fear of putting on weight. But it is the type of fats that they consume that makes them unhealthy – uncooked fats are metabolised by the body in a different way, and are essential for good health. Fats are a vital part of the diet, particularly the essential fatty acids.

We need nuts and seeds, including coconut and cacao, avocados, olives and their oils. The best sources of essential fatty acids are flaxseed, hemp seed and chia.

CALCIUM

In one tablespoon of sesame seeds, there is more than eight times the amount of calcium than there is in a cup of cow's milk! Weight for weight, green leafy vegetables contain roughly double the amount of calcium as cow's milk.

All nuts and seeds, especially sesame, flax, hazelnuts, almonds, brazils. Chick peas, garlic, figs, and leafy greens. All sea vegetables, especially dulse and kelp.

PHOSPHOROUS

All nuts and seeds, especially pumpkin seeds. Buckwheat, quinoa, rye, wheat, and sea vegetables.

MAGNESIUM

All nuts and seeds, especially pumpkin seeds. Buckwheat, rye. Sea vegetables. Cacao.

POTASSIUM

Grains, especially buckwheat, quinoa, rye, and wheat. Chick peas, lentils, mung beans. All nuts and seeds, especially pistachios. Avocados, bananas, dates, raisins. Parsley, spinach. Sea vegetables.

IRON

30 g/1 oz of flaxseed contains more than double the RDA of iron.

Quinoa, nuts and seeds, especially flaxseed, pumpkin seeds, sesame seeds. All leafy greens especially parsley. Sea vegetables.

COPPER

Nuts and seeds, especially pecans and walnuts. Buckwheat.

ZINC

Buckwheat, quinoa, miso, all nuts and seeds especially pumpkin seeds and sesame seeds. Leafy greens.

CHROMIUM

Wheat, apples, broccoli, corn, mushrooms, onion, pears.

SELENIUM

Brazil nuts.

VITAMIN A

Apricots, melons, papaya, sharon fruit, beetroot, broccoli, carrots, leafy greens, sweet potato, goji berries. Nori.

VITAMIN C

All fruits and vegetables, especially guavas, kiwi, papaya, strawberries, blackcurrants, broccoli, cauliflower, peppers, kale.

B VITAMINS

Leafy greens, nutritional yeast flakes, sea vegetables, goji berries, bee pollen.

B12

There is some controversy over how a healthy vegan gets their B12. My understanding is that there are small amounts of bioavailable B12 in fermented foods and drinks, and also in bee products such as pollen and royal jelly, but not enough to rely on. I would recommend supplementation, to be safe. The best kind of supplements are the sublingual sprays that go under the tongue and straight into the bloodstream.

VITAMIN D

There are no vegan sources of vitamin D. You need approximately 100 hours a year of direct, full body sunlight a year to metabolise enough vitamin D in the body – you don't need me to tell you we don't get that much in the UK! So some raw fooders choose to include small amounts of raw dairy produce in order to get this essential vitamin. If you're a strict vegan, then you need to supplement – it's vitamin D3 you want, and again, the best form to take it in is the sublingual sprays.

VITAMIN E

Almonds, brazil nuts, hazelnuts, cucumber.

ABOUT THE RECIPES

Each and every recipe here is a dish that I have regularly served my family over the past decade. Although some are more time-consuming than others, and many require advance preparation, none are so labour intensive as to be unrealistic to incorporate into your daily menu. All quantities given have worked for me, but with raw foods there are no hard and fast rules; you can vary ingredients wherever you choose, for instance substituting one vegetable for another, or one nut for another. Or if you are particularly fond of an ingredient, you can add extra to suit your taste e.g. more garlic, extra almonds. Some raw food tastes are 'acquired'; as your taste buds become attuned to this way of eating, you can experiment with some of the more unusual dishes. Keep an open mind, and don't expect it to taste the same as cooked food – raw pizza, for example, is a real treat for us, but only a distant cousin to the high street version. Raw foods are packed with goodness, no empty calories, and so are often more intense in their flavour; you may well find you need to eat much smaller portions to feel full. Many dishes suit being left for 24-48 hours, as the flavours meld together, so it's a good idea to make more than you need and re-use it the next day. This also means you're not constantly creating mealtimes from scratch. Be creative: what serves as a salad dressing one day can be used as a spread for crackers the next. Leftover pasta sauce? Put it on bread and make a pizza. Too much smoothie? Dehydrate it and make a dried fruit snack to give the kids next time you are out for the day. All leftovers should be stored in the fridge, with the exception of dehydrated goodies, which must be kept in an airtight container.

Breakfasts

CINNAMON BUCKWHEAT
PORRIDGE

MISO BUCKWHEAT PORRIDGE

GOJI AND COCONUT MUESLI

COCONUT AND
MACA PORRIDGE

CHIA PORRIDGE

CARROT AND GARLIC
PORRIDGE

CINNAMON BUCKWHEAT PORRIDGE

If you have a cook's thermometer, you can warm the porridges, making sure the temperature stays below 42°C / 108°F. You will need to add extra water gradually, while stirring continuously. You can also do this in a porringer or Thermomix.

250 g/8 oz sprouted buckwheat
  (see page 18)
1 tbsp tahini
1 tsp cinnamon
1 tbsp agave
2 tbsp raisins
2 tbsp hot water
1 tbsp sunflower seeds, soaked
1 tbsp pumpkin seeds, soaked

Pre-soak your seeds for at least an hour. In the food processor, break down the buckwheat until the grains are a creamy mash. Add the tahini, cinnamon, and agave and process again to make a thick batter. While the machine is running, pour in the water and process for a further minute. Turn the machine off, and stir in the raisins, pumpkin seeds and sunflower seeds with a spoon. Serve immediately, while warm.

Someone who doesn't have so many toxins in their system wakes in the morning with plenty of energy, and no immediate desire for food. The digestive system doesn't really get going until midday, so the later in the morning you can leave it before eating, the easier it is on your body.

Serves 2 // Takes 5 minutes, just remember to sprout the buckwheat first
You need a food processor or blender

MISO BUCKWHEAT PORRIDGE

Although porridge is traditionally made with oats, this buckwheat mash is a first class alternative. I discovered this when making buckwheat biscuits – the mixture was just as appetizing as the finished version!

250 g/8 oz sprouted buckwheat
  (see page 18)
1 tbsp extra virgin olive oil
1 tsp miso
2 tbsp fresh parsley, chopped
  finely
¼ red onion, chopped finely
2 tbsp hot water
1 tbsp pumpkin seeds, soaked
1 tbsp sunflower seeds, soaked

Remember to sprout your buckwheat in advance. Pre-soak your seeds for at least an hour. In the food processor, break down the buckwheat until it forms a creamy mash. Add the extra virgin olive oil, miso, parsley and onion, and process again to make a thick batter. Next, pour in the water and blend until you have a creamy puree. Turn the machine off, and stir in the pumpkin and sunflower seeds with a spoon. Serve immediately.

Buckwheat is actually a herb; the part that we sprout is the seed. Despite the name, buckwheat is not related to wheat, and doesn't contain gluten. It's also very alkalising.

Serves 2 // Takes 5 minutes, just remember to sprout the buckwheat first
You need a food processor or blender

GOJI AND COCONUT MUESLI

A lot of raw fooders don't eat breakfast, so we are more likely to serve these dishes as a snack or brunch. My boys enjoy a hearty breakfast like this; I prefer to just have liquids like juice, milk or tea.

45 g/1½ oz wheat sprouts
   (see page 18) or raw oats,
   soaked 4-8 hours
2 tbsp sunflower sprouts
   (see page 18)
2 tbsp raisins
1 tbsp shelled hemp seeds
1 tbsp coconut flakes
1 tbsp goji berries
1 tbsp dates, chopped

Stir all the ingredients together until they are thoroughly mixed, and serve with almond milk (page 153).

You will find it easier to cut dried fruit into small pieces with scissors, rather than using a knife. Not all coconut flakes are raw; check with your supplier.

Serves 2
Takes 5 minutes, plus time for sprouting or pre-soaking
You don't need any equipment

COCONUT AND MACA PORRIDGE

Rolled oats that are used in porridge are always heated during the processing. Oat groats are simply the hulled grain; they are not raw either. They are about the same size as rice grains, and must be soaked for 8-12 hours, although they do not sprout. At Raw Living we have sourced raw oats straight from the farmer. They are a lot creamier and nuttier, although they only keep for a few weeks.

125 g/4 oz raw oats, soaked at
   least 2 hours
1 tbsp agave
1 tbsp coconut oil
1 tsp cinnamon
125 ml/4 fl oz hot water
2 tbsp raisins
2 tbsp coconut flakes
2 tsp maca powder

Remember to pre-soak your oats. Put them in the food processor and process for a couple of minutes, until the individual grains are no longer discernible, and they have formed a thick mash. Add the agave, coconut oil and cinnamon, and blend again. Then pour in the water, and process to a thick creamy puree. Turn the machine off, and stir in the raisins, coconut and maca powder with a spoon. Serve immediately, while warm.

Maca is a Peruvian root vegetable which is known for providing energy and stamina. It makes a great breakfast food and combines well with oats. It has a sweet malty flavour.

Serves 2 // Takes 5 minutes and you need to pre-soak your oats 2-4 hours
You need a food processor or blender

CARROT AND GARLIC PORRIDGE

This makes a warming and sustaining brunch on a cold winter's day. No point trying to do fruit salad for breakfast in December, or it won't be long before you are reaching for the bread! Better to have a big hearty raw breakfast that will keep you happy all morning.

125 g/4 oz raw oats, soaked 2 hours
1 tbsp carrot, grated
1 clove garlic
1 tbsp fresh parsley, chopped finely
1 tsp miso
1 tbsp flaxseed oil
125 ml/4 fl oz hot water

Pre-soak your oats for 2-4 hours. Put the oats in the food processor, and process for a couple of minutes, until the individual grains are no longer discernible, but have formed a thick mash. Add all other ingredients apart from water, and process for a further minute. Then pour in the water, and keep the machine turning until you have a creamy batter. Serve immediately.

Serves 2
Takes 5 minutes, with 2-4 hours pre-soaking
You need a food processor or blender

Garlic, miso, and oats together give terrific protection against winter illnesses. Garlic was eaten by Roman gladiators to improve their strength in the stadium.

Chia was a staple food of the Aztecs and Mayans. It was given to them as rations while they were on long marches, as it was known to be so good for energy and stamina.

CHIA PORRIDGE

Chia is a very popular breakfast food. It's a South American seed which has only been available in the UK since around 2010, so it's new to a lot of people. When you soak chia, it absorbs up to four times its volume in water, which makes it very economical, and a handy food to take with you on the road. It's a great source of energy and protein, plus it's one of the very best sources of those all important EFAs, particularly the hard to find Omega 3s.

125 g/4 oz chia
1 litre/32 fl oz milk (see below)
150 g/5 oz raisins
150 g/5 oz fresh fruit

Soak the chia in milk. I recommend almond milk (page 153), but you could use soya milk, rice milk, goats' milk, or whichever milk you favour. Stir in the raisins, and some chopped fresh fruit. Again, this is down to your own personal preference, and what is in season. You might choose apples, bananas, pears, strawberries, peaches, apricots....the possibilities are endless. Cover, and leave for at least 4 hours to soak. Many people like to make it before bed and then it's ready for breakfast in the morning. Keeps in the fridge for up to five days.

Serves 4
Takes 10 minutes, with minimum 4 hours pre-soaking
You don't need any special equipment

Soups

TOMATO AND BASIL SOUP

SHIITAKE MUSHROOM
SOUP

SUNSHINE SOUP

THAI SOUP

CREAMY CARROT
AND SPINACH SOUP

CREAM OF
COCONUT SOUP

TOMATO AND BASIL SOUP

Adding the avocado makes for a creamier soup.

6 tomatoes
½ stick celery
1 clove garlic
2 dates
1 tbsp fresh basil
1 tbsp nutritional yeast
   flakes
1 tsp liquid aminos
125 ml/4 fl oz water
½ avocado (optional)

Prepare your vegetables for the blender.
Put everything in together, and puree until smooth.

Serves 2 // Takes 10 minutes
You need a blender

Soups can be warmed gently, either by using hot water where water is stated in the recipe, or by heating in a porringer, using a cook's thermometer to check the temperature (no more than 42°C/ 108°F). None of these soups suit being heated to boiling point.

SHIITAKE MUSHROOM SOUP

The shiitake mushrooms add a real depth of flavour to this soup.
Shiitake are very high in a polysaccharide known as beta-glucans that
is exceptionally beneficial for the immune system.

60 g/2 oz shiitake
   mushrooms
6 chestnut mushrooms
½ red pepper
2 tbsp fresh parsley
2 tbsp almond butter
1 tsp miso
1 tbsp flaxseed oil
375 ml/12 fl oz water

Roughly chop the mushrooms and pepper to prepare them for the blender. Put everything in and blend to a smooth puree.

Serves 2
Takes 10 minutes
You need a blender

Shiitake mushrooms have immune system boosting properties, and have been used in the treatment of AIDS. There are many other kinds of medicinal mushrooms used widely in the raw food community that you might like to experiment with such as Reishi, cordyceps and chaga.

SUNSHINE SOUP

A basic recipe – you can vary it with your own favourite vegetables. (Picture opposite)

3 tomatoes
1 yellow pepper
½ avocado
60 g/2 oz spinach
250 ml/8 fl oz carrot juice
1 tbsp flaxseed oil
1 tsp miso
1 cm/½ inch piece fresh
   ginger
1 clove garlic
½ red chilli pepper

Prepare the tomatoes, pepper, avocado and spinach for the blender. Put everything in together, and puree until all ingredients have been broken down and you have a smooth, lump-free soup.

Serves 2 // Takes 10 minutes // You need a blender

Tomatoes contain lycopene, an antioxidant which helps protect against cancer. The darker the tomato, the higher its lycopene content.

THAI SOUP

This is one to serve to impress your guests! If you can't get fresh coconut you can use 250 ml/8 fl oz of coconut milk instead, but coconut milk is not raw.

3 mushrooms
3 tomatoes
1 clove garlic
0.5 cm/ ¼ inch piece fresh ginger
0.5 cm/¼ inch piece galangal
½ lemon grass stick
1 red chilli pepper
2 dates
3 lime leaves
juice 1 lime
small bunch coriander
60 g/2 oz fresh brown coconut,
   chopped
125 g/4 oz spinach
½ apple
1 tsp tamari
water to blend

Chop the mushrooms and tomatoes ready for the blender. Put everything in together, and puree thoroughly for a couple of minutes, making sure there are no bits of herb or spice left unprocessed. Serve garnished with sprouts such as mung bean or lentil.

I really missed Thai food for a while, until I realised that the secret was all in the delicate balance of the flavours, and that I would be able to recreate that in a raw dish, using the same ingredients. Thai dishes are usually only lightly cooked anyway, so as not to destroy the exquisite balance of tastes.

Serves 2 // Takes 15 minutes // You need a blender

CREAMY CARROT AND SPINACH SOUP

Carrot and spinach soup was a favourite of mine when I ate cooked food.
The sweetness of the carrots complements the slightly bitter spinach perfectly.

3 large carrots, chopped
180 g/6 oz spinach
1/4 red onion
1 clove garlic
½ apple, chopped
1 avocado
1 tsp miso
1 tbsp flaxseed oil
1 tsp kelp powder
250 ml/8 fl oz hot water
45 g/ 1½ oz mung bean sprouts
  (see page 18)

Prepare all your veggies for the blender. Put everything in apart from the sprouts and puree until smooth. Mix the sprouts in by hand - sprinkle a few on the top as a garnish.

Spinach is a first rate source of iron; two out of three women in the UK are iron deficient.

Serves 2 // Takes 10 minutes // You need a blender

CREAM OF COCONUT SOUP

This is a very rich, warming soup. I practically lived on it for a good while about twenty years ago. Like all raw soups, it is so quick and easy to prepare (just as quick as heating up the contents of a can!). The richness of the coconut contrasts beautifully with the sharpness of the celery and carrot.

90 g/3 oz creamed coconut
½ red chilli
1 clove garlic
0.5 cm/¼ inch piece fresh ginger
¼ red onion
2 dates
250 ml/8 fl oz hot water
30 g/1 oz lentil sprouts (see page
  18)
1 stick celery, sliced thinly
1 carrot, sliced thinly

Fine slice the celery and carrots; using a mandolin would be good if you have one. Put everything apart from the sprouts, celery, and carrot into the blender. Blend for a couple of minutes until you have a thick puree. Transfer to a bowl, and using a spoon, stir the sprouts, celery, and carrot into the coconut sauce.

You can make your own creamed coconut, follow the method for nut butter on page 38. In the USA, a product labelled coconut butter is actually more similiar to what we would term creamed coconut. If you can find a product which is the whole coconut pressed, rather than just the oil, you could use that instead. For instance, currently Nutiva make one called Coconut Manna.

Serves 1 // Takes 10 minutes // You need a blender

Nut Butters, Dips, Dressings and Sauces

NUT BUTTERS

Conventional nut and seed butters are never raw, but instead usually roasted. The oils in nuts and seeds are notoriously unstable so heating preserves them and stops them going rancid. Unfortunately, many of the raw brands sold in the UK are rancid! If you buy a jar and it tastes bitter or has a strange aftertaste, take it back to the store where you bought it. My favourite brand is Sun & Seed, I have never had a problem with any of theirs and they have a wide range, including hemp, pumpkin, almond, walnut and tahini.

If you want to make your own, you can break down nuts in a high power blender or food processor, and although they become more homogenized than ground nuts, they don't really qualify as nut butter. If you're just adding them to recipes e.g. soups and sweets, it works fine, but they don't have the flavour or the texture of commercial nut butters if you're looking to spread them on crackers or breads. Tahini and almond butter are staples. Brazils and macadamias work very well (probably because they are already heat-treated).

Put the nuts or seeds in the machine and turn it on maximum speed, stopping regularly to stir it and make sure it is evenly mixed. As the nuts and seeds break down, the friction in the machine will cause them to heat up, which is obviously undesirable. Once it starts to get warm, turn it off and leave for half an hour to an hour, then return to it, and process again. Repeat this process throughout the day. Gradually, it should turn from a powder to a paste, and finally a butter. The longer you persevere with it, the runnier the end result. Store in the fridge.

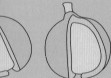

CRAZY CARROT DIP

This makes a thick, zesty dip or spread. It's so superb you can just eat it as it is!
I use it in roll-ups (page 86), or as a dip with raw vegetables.

3 carrots
¼ red onion
2 tbsp chopped fresh dill
2 tbsp lemon juice
1 tbsp tamari
2 tbsp extra virgin olive oil
4 tbsp tahini
2 tbsp water

Prepare your carrot and onion for the blender. Put everything in together and blend for a couple of minutes until you have a smooth puree.

A friend inspired this dish when she told me that she makes dips simply by blending up whatever raw vegetables she has to hand with some tahini. This is the best combination I have found, and I often make it when I have a lot of people visiting, as it is economical and easy to make in bulk.

Makes 8 servings // Takes 10 minutes // You need a blender

Picture opposite: front, broccoli and rosemary dip, crazy carrot dip and red hot pepper dip

REUBEN'S DIP

I made this for my son when he was a toddler as it's packed full of nourishment. He used to have it spread on gluten-free bread, or as a dip for cucumber and carrot sticks. Add water to reach the desired consistency – a little will give you a very thick spread. Add a little more if you're using it as a dip, and more again to make a nutritious, creamy salad dressing.

3 tbsp tahini
1 tbsp miso
2 tbsp nutritional yeast flakes
2 tbsp flaxseeds, ground
1 tbsp apple cider vinegar
1 tsp kelp powder
water

Grind your flaxseeds, if you haven't already. Put everything in a small bowl, and using a hand whisk, blend it all together.

Miso is a Japanese food, used in macrobiotic cookery. It's traditionally made from fermented soya beans and/or rice, is full of enzymes and B vitamins, and is effective at warding off illness. Try stirring a teaspoon into a cup of boiling water to make a warming savoury drink. There is an excellent English make from Source foods, or Clearspring import high quality miso from Japan. Look for unpasteurised miso as that has all the enzymatic activity intact; pasteurisation destroys the enzymes.

Makes 8 servings // Takes 10 minutes // No special equipment needed

BEST GUACAMOLE

Guacamole is one raw dish that everyone has heard of and a staple for raw fooders. Most raw fooders (us included) eat avocados every day as an essential source of monounsaturated fats in the diet. Guacamole is very versatile: spread it on crackers, use it as a dip for raw vegetables, or add it to roll-ups (page 86).

1 large avocado
1 tomato
1 tbsp red onion
1 tbsp fresh coriander
1 tbsp fresh parsley
1 garlic clove
1 tsp kelp powder
½ red chilli pepper
1 tsp tamari
juice 1 lemon

Roughly chop the avocado and tomato. Blend everything except the tamari and lemon juice in the food processor. When you have no lumps left, add the tamari and lemon juice, and process for a further minute, until the mixture starts to thicken.

If you're preparing guacamole in advance, store it with an avocado stone in it to prevent it turning an unappetising brown colour.

Serves 4 // Takes 15 minutes // You need a food processor

RED HOT PEPPER DIP

This makes a vibrant, spicy dip or spread. Great for crackers, crudités and roll-ups (page 86).
You'll be amazed how liquid peppers turn when you blend them up.

3 red peppers
1 stick celery
150 g/5 oz tahini
1 tsp ground cumin
1 tbsp tamari
2 tbsp extra virgin olive oil
1 clove garlic
1 red chilli pepper

Prepare the peppers and celery for the blender. Put everything in together and process for a couple of minutes until you have a thick puree.

Cumin is a spice commonly used in curry powder, but I use it frequently on its own to add an Indian flavour to a dish.

Makes 4 servings // Takes 10 minutes // You need a blender

HAPPY RAW HUMMUS

If you love hummus, try this raw version, which uses the same ingredients, but
made from sprouted chick peas rather than cooked ones. Raw chick peas are quite
difficult to digest so eat this with a simple salad or vegetable dips –
avoid mixing with crackers or crisps unless you have very efficient digestion.

250 g/8 oz sprouted chick peas
  (see page 18)
2 tbsp tahini
2 tbsp extra virgin olive oil
1 tbsp lemon juice
1 tsp tamari
2 cloves garlic
2 tbsp water

Make sure you've already sprouted your chick peas. Put everything in the blender, and blend for couple of minutes until you have a thick puree.

If you fancy a snack lunch, any of the dips in this section make a delicious light meal served with an array of crudités such as mushroom, broccoli, cucumber, carrot, or pepper. Good for packed lunches.

Serves 4 // Takes 15 minutes, don't forget to sprout your chick peas in advance
You need a blender

'There's rosemary, that's for remembrance' is a line from Shakespeare's Hamlet; scientists have shown that rosemary does actually act as a stimulant to the memory.

BROCCOLI AND ROSEMARY DIP

The rosemary adds an unusual tang to this recipe, which goes well in nori rolls (page 86), or spread on crackers.

1 large head broccoli (250 g/8 oz)
¼ red onion
1 avocado
2 sprigs rosemary
½ tsp rock salt
2 tbsp extra virgin olive oil
1 lime, juiced
½ tsp cayenne pepper

Prepare the broccoli, onion, and avocado for the blender or food processor. Remove the rosemary leaves from the stem; discard the stem. Blend everything for a couple of minutes. If you like a bit of texture, you can leave it a bit lumpy with the broccoli discernible; or you can process longer until it is a smooth puree.

Serves 4 // Takes 10 minutes
You need a blender or food processor

BALSAMIC MUSHROOM PÂTÉ

This is fantastic on crackers such as Raw-vita (page 56) or garlic crackers (page 54).

8 mushrooms
1 stick celery
small bunch parsley
1 clove garlic
½ red chilli pepper
1 tsp miso
1 tbsp balsamic vinegar
60 g/2 oz sunflower
   seeds, soaked
90 g/3 oz sesame seeds,
   soaked
2 tbsp olive oil
2 tbsp water

Make sure you've pre-
soaked your sunflower
and pumpkin seeds for
2-4 hours. Prepare the
mushrooms, celery and
parsley for the food processor.
Put in everything apart from the
water, and process until smooth.
Pour in the water gradually, and when
it's fully blended in, it's ready to serve.

Serves 4
Takes 10 minutes, with 2-4 hours pre-soaking
time
You need a food processor

TERRIFIC TAHINI DIP

This is simple but very palatable – suitable for when you're in a hurry, or have to cater for large groups. If you're a garlic fan, add some, crushed. It makes a wonderful spread for crackers or creamy dip for crudités. The magic of this spread is that you can make twice as much tahini out of a jar, as the lemon juice thickens it so much you have to add a lot of water to make it runny again. Plus the lemon makes the tahini easier to digest.

250 g/8 oz tahini
2 tbsp lemon juice
1 tbsp tamari
4 tbsp water

Blend everything in the food processor, or manually with a hand whisk.

Made from ground sesame seeds, tahini is very high in calcium, and an essential part of a raw vegan diet. It has a neutral taste that goes well with sweet and savoury dishes, and can be used in place of butter and margarine as a spread.

Serves 8 // Takes 10 minutes
No special equipment needed

SPICY SUNFLOWER PÂTÉ

You can use any combination of vegetables that you have to hand
e.g. broccoli, mushroom, celery, carrot. Or replace the sunflower seeds
with 125 g/4 oz pumpkin seeds, soaked overnight.

300 g/10 oz mixed vegetables
small bunch parsley
¼ red onion
125 g/4 oz sunflower seeds,
   soaked 2-4 hours
2 tbsp flaxseed oil
2 tbsp lemon juice
1 tbsp tamari
1 tsp ground cumin
½ red chilli pepper
1 clove garlic

Soak your sunflower seeds for 2-4 hours. Prepare the vegetables, parsley and onion, so they are ready for your food processor. Put everything in the food processor, and mix for a couple of minutes until it is a smooth puree.

This can be used as a dip, to make roll-ups (page 86), or it's particularly agreeable when stuffed in peppers.

Serves 4
Takes 15 minutes, and pre-soak your
sunflower seeds for 2-4 hours
You need a food processor

TOMATO KETCHUP

This is first class – you can use it as a dip or a salad dressing (see page 78), not just as an accompaniment to burgers and sausages.

3 tomatoes
½ red onion
60 g/2 oz dried tomatoes
4 dates
1 tbsp apple cider vinegar
1 tsp tamari
1 tsp kelp powder

Prepare the tomatoes and onion for the blender. Put everything in together, and puree until smooth.

I find my dehydrator invaluable for making dried tomatoes, which add depth to any tomato dish. If you can't dry your own, you can buy them in packets. I wouldn't recommend using tomato puree; it's not raw, and when used in large amounts, such as in this recipe, it can have an unpleasant, metallic, processed taste.

Serves 4 // Takes 10 minutes // You need a blender

ULTIMATE DRESSING

This has everything in it! It makes the creamiest, yummiest dressing ever. It makes quite a lot so you can store it in the fridge and use for a few salads, or as a creamy sauce over vegetables. Experiment with different herbs to see which you favour.

bunch parsley
2 tbsp fresh tarragon/basil/dill –
   whatever you fancy
¼ red onion
60 g/2 oz almond butter
½ avocado
2 tbsp extra virgin olive oil
1 tbsp tamari
1 tbsp lemon juice
1 tbsp apple cider vinegar
1 tbsp nutritional yeast flakes
1 tsp kelp powder
125 ml/4 fl oz water

Put everything in the blender together and process for a few minutes until the mixture starts to thicken.

Dill is my favourite herb. It has a distinctive refreshing flavour that can transform an average dish into something more memorable. It is said to be very beneficial for the digestion, and a help to IBS sufferers.

Serves 8
Takes 10 minutes
You need a blender

UMEBOSHI DRESSING

Umeboshi paste is a very pungent, salty substance, made from Japanese pickled plums.
It is very alkalising, good for the digestion and is used in macrobiotic cookery.
This dressing will add a distinctive tang to any salad.

2 tsp umeboshi paste
1 tbsp tahini
1 tbsp nutritional yeast flakes
1 tbsp flaxseed oil
½ tsp kelp powder
water to mix

Put everything in a small bowl, and blend together with a hand whisk. Add water drop by drop to reach desired consistency.

Kelp seaweed is sold in powder or granular form, and has a salty, fishy taste. It has the highest mineral count of any food and is particularly important as a source of iodine. Try and get some seaweed in your diet every day by adding just half a teaspoon of kelp to your dinner.

Serves 2 // Takes 5 minutes // No equipment needed

NIKKI'S DRESSING

Nikki first made this dressing for me in 1995, and in doing so introduced me to the wonderful buttery flavour of flaxseed oil. Back then it was a hard to find ingredient and I had never tasted it before. I think Nikki had just been to the USA and discovered it there. Flax oil adds depth and richness whenever it is used in a dish. It is very sensitive to heat and light, and can be found in the chiller cabinet of health food stores. Although it is expensive, it is an essential addition to your diet being one of the few sources of essential fatty acids (the other main dietary source is fish).

1 avocado, mashed
1 tbsp flaxseed oil
1 tsp liquid aminos
1 tbsp nutritional yeast flakes
1 tsp kelp powder
1 tbsp water

Put everything in a bowl, and blend together with a hand whisk.

If your avocados are unripe, put them in a paper bag and leave them on the windowsill to ripen them quickly. Even better, put a banana in the bag with them. This works with most fruits.

Serves 2
Takes 5 minutes
No equipment needed

EASY AVO MAYO

This is an easy alternative to mayonnaise which you can knock up in a couple of minutes.

1 large avocado
2 tbsp lemon juice
1 tsp apple cider vinegar
1 tsp tamari

Prepare the avocado for the blender. Put everything in the blender or food processor, and blend for a few minutes until mixture thickens to the same consistency as egg mayonnaise.

The longer the avocado is, the smaller its stone will be. Fatter avocados often have bigger stones, and are not necessarily the best buy. My favourite avocados are the Reed avocados you find in California.

AWESOME ALMOND MAYO

This takes slightly longer to prepare than the previous recipe, but is more authentic.

125 g/4 oz almonds, soaked
  4-8 hours
250 ml/8 fl oz water
1 lemon, juiced
1 tsp tamari
¼ red onion, chopped
1 tbsp apple cider vinegar
1 fresh date

Pre-soak your almonds for 4-8 hours; this makes them more digestible. Put everything in the blender, and process for a few minutes until the mixture thickens to the same consistency as egg mayonnaise. It will thicken further when stored in the fridge.

Most of what we call nuts actually fall under other classifications: almonds are a fruit, for instance, and peanuts are a legume.

Serves 8 // Takes 10 minutes to make, with 4-8 hours pre-soaking
You need a blender

SATAY SAUCE

This is a fantastic sauce; I particularly like it as a dip for broccoli and mushroom, or you can use it as a dip for spring rolls. Satay sauce is traditionally made from peanuts, but peanuts are not healthy for a number of reasons: they are extremely hard on the digestion, and are prone to a potentially carcinogenic fungus.

60 g/2 oz dates
125 g/4 oz almonds, soaked 4-8
  hours
1 red chilli pepper, finely chopped
1 tsp tamari
juice 1 lemon
4 tbsp water
4 tbsp extra virgin olive oil

Make sure you've pre-soaked the almonds. Break down the dates in the food processor until they form a homogenised mass. Add the soaked almonds and chilli, and process until you have a paste. Lastly, add the tamari, lemon juice and water, and puree until creamy.

I always use fresh chillies in preference to chilli powder. They cost a few pence, and have more flavour than the dried powder. Remove the seeds, because these are what cause your mouth to burn. If you prefer to use dried chilli powder ¼ fresh chilli is roughly equivalent to ½ tsp chilli powder.

Serves 4 // Takes 15 minutes to make, with 4-8 hours pre-soaking
You need a food processor

BBQ SAUCE

Use as a dip, a dressing, or a sauce for burgers.

3 tomatoes
1 tsp miso
1 tbsp yacon syrup or raw honey
1 red chilli pepper, finely chopped
1 clove garlic
1 tbsp olive oil
6 sun-dried tomatoes

Prepare the tomatoes for the blender. Put everything in together, and blend until smooth.

Yacon syrup comes from South America and is a unique sweetener which actually has no impact on the blood sugar, so is suitable for diabetics and people on anti-candida diets. The only other sweetener suitable for diabetics is stevia, which just became legal in the EU in 2012.

Serves 4 // Takes 10 minutes // You need a blender

THE BEST SALSA

Everyone is familiar with salsa as a dip; the word is actually Spanish for sauce. When it's freshly made, it's first rate, and makes a delightful salad in its own right.

small bunch coriander
1/4 red onion
1/2 red chilli pepper
juice 1/2 lemon
1 tsp miso
1 tbsp extra virgin olive oil
1 tsp agave
6 tomatoes, cubed

In the food processor, blend thoroughly all ingredients apart from tomatoes – just add one tomato into the blender. Add the tomatoes, process for a few seconds only, or chop them and stir them in by hand, so that they are thoroughly incorporated into the mixture but still retain their chunkiness.

'Vegetables' that are horticulturally defined as fruits include cucumbers, peppers, tomatoes, courgettes, aubergines, marrow, avocados and olives.

Serves 2 // Takes 10 minutes
You need a blender or food processor

TAHINI AND MISO GRAVY

Serve over burgers, nut loaf, or use as a dressing or dip. This has a rich, almost alcoholic flavour.

2 tbsp tahini
1 tbsp miso
2 tbsp extra virgin olive oil
2 dates
1/4 red onion
2 tbsp water
1 tomato

Put everything in the blender and puree until you get a thick sauce.

If you can find a plentiful and inexpensive supply, use fresh dates in my recipes in preference to dried dates, which may not be raw, and often have less flavour. If you're using dried dates you may have to soak them for 20 minutes to an hour to soften them up. Drink the soak water – it is delightfully sweet, and full of nutrients.

Serves 4 // Takes 10 minutes // You need a blender

FAMOUS PASTA SAUCE

This is one of my favourite recipes. I have been making it regularly for over 10 years. I have demonstrated it all over the world, it's been in countless magazines, and even on TV. If you love pasta, you can drown it in this nutritious sauce and make it a really healthy meal. I would try to avoid wheat; you can get excellent wheat-free pastas in the health food stores, made from grains such as corn, buckwheat, rice, and spelt.

3 tomatoes
½ avocado
2 carrots
1 stick celery
6 sun-dried tomatoes
2 fresh dates
¼ red onion
2 tbsp extra virgin olive oil
1 tsp tamari
1 tbsp apple cider vinegar
2 tbsp fresh basil
1 clove garlic
½ red chilli pepper

Prepare the tomatoes, avocado, carrots and celery for the blender. Put everything in the blender and blend to a thick sauce.

This was the children's favourite dinner for a good many years. I don't eat cooked pasta, so I either just eat the sauce as it is, as a dip for raw vegetables, or make raw 'pasta' by peeling vegetables such as carrot and courgette with a vegetable peeler. You can also buy a piece of equipment called a Spiralizer especially for the purpose, which does a fantastically quick and easy job of making noodles from vegetables such as courgettes and carrots.

Serves 2 // Takes 15 minutes // You need a blender

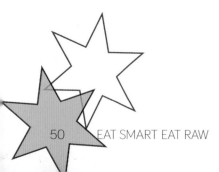

The cashews that we commonly come across are never raw, as they are heated to remove the shell. You can get truly raw ones, but they are extremely hard to come by – check the specialist raw stores online.

GRATED 'CHEESE'

Serve sprinkled over a pasta dish, as a garnish for soup, or use to liven up a salad.

60 g/2 oz cashew nuts
2 tbsp nutritional yeast flakes
1 tbsp nori flakes

Break cashews down in a grinder or a food processor until the pieces are small lumps the size of grated cheese. By hand, mix the nuts with the flakes, until they are thoroughly coated. A drop or two of water may help the flakes to stick.

Serves 4 // Takes 5 minutes // You need a food processor

MELTED 'CHEESE'

For pizzas, or spread on crackers.

60 g/2 oz ground flaxseed
2 tbsp nutritional yeast flakes
1 tbsp tamari
2 tbsp water

Serves 4 // Takes 10 minutes
You don't need any special
equipment

Grind your flaxseeds. Using a spoon, mix everything together, adding water gradually to make a thick paste. It will thicken further when stored; you may want to add more water to make it runnier.

I adore this; it has exactly the same sort of elasticity as melted cheese. What I love about raw recipes, is that their starting point is healthy, nutritious ingredients, food that will do you good – food as medicine, if you like. But because the food is so alive, they end up tasting so yummy, that you want to eat them just for their fantastic flavours, and the nutritional value becomes secondary.

Snacks and Side Dishes

GARLIC CRACKERS

PIZZA CRACKERS

DULSE CRACKERS

HUMMUS CRACKERS

RAW-VITA

TOMATO CRISPS

KALE CHIPS

'ROASTED' NUTS

SPRING ROLLS

STUFFED MUSHROOMS

'CHEESY' STUFFED PEPPERS

DILL STUFFED PEPPERS

STUFFED AVOCADO

FALAFEL

ONION BHAJIS

CURRIED SPINACH

MARINATED MUSHROOMS

'COOKED' BUCKWHEAT

GARLIC CRACKERS

If you are making crackers in the dehydrator, you need to cover the mesh trays with something to stop the mixture sticking. You can buy special teflex sheets, designed for the purpose, or you can buy similar paraflex sheets in the supermarket and cut them to size. If you have neither, you can use greaseproof paper.

300 g/10 oz buckwheat, sprouted (see page 18)
2 tbsp cashews, ground
2 tbsp flaxseed, ground
4 cloves garlic
1 tbsp tamari
small bunch parsley
2 tbsp water

Remember to sprout your buckwheat. Make sure you've ground your cashews and flaxseeds in advance. Put everything except the water in the food processor. Process for a couple of minutes until all the ingredients have formed a thick batter. Keep the machine on, and add water gradually, processing for a further minute. Then spread into thin cracker shapes around 8-10 cm (3-4 inch) in diameter, and dehydrate for about 12 hours until crispy.

For **nori crackers** replace parsley with 2 tbsp nori flakes. Savoury crackers are unbeatable spread with avocado and smothered in alfalfa. Or try any of the dips from the first section, topped with a selection of lettuce, tomato, alfalfa, etc.

Makes about 25 crackers // Takes 20 minutes, plus time to sprout your buckwheat, and 12 hours dehydrating // You need a food processor and a dehydrator

PIZZA CRACKERS

Most dehydrator crackers keep indefinitely if stored in an airtight container – a good three months if properly dried. The recipes in this section make quite large amounts so you can keep them in storage and not have to keep making them.

180 g/6 oz sprouted wheat (see page 18)
large handful fresh herbs e.g. basil, rosemary, parsley, thyme, oregano
4 cloves garlic
4 tomatoes
2 tbsp nutritional yeast flakes
1 tbsp tamari
2 tbsp extra virgin olive oil

Sprout your wheat in advance. Mash the wheat grain in a food processor (it won't break down completely). Add the herbs and garlic, and process until they are thoroughly mixed in. Next, add the tomatoes and blend them in. Then add the remaining ingredients and process for a minute more, until you have a thick batter. On dehydrator sheets, spread the batter into thin cracker shapes around 8-10 cm (3-4 inch) in diameter, and dehydrate for about 12 hours, until crunchy. Store in an airtight container; it will keep for a few weeks.

You can make this into two large rounds instead of individual crackers and use as pizza bases.

Makes about 25 crackers // Takes 20 minutes to make, with time for sprouting wheat in advance and 12 hours dehydrating // You need a food processor or high power blender, plus a dehydrator

DULSE CRACKERS

These crackers are as delicious as they are nutritious. Dulse is one of the easiest sea vegetables to use as it doesn't need any pre-soaking, and doesn't have the same strong taste that some people don't enjoy about the other sea vegetables.

125 g/4 oz rolled oats, pre-soaked 4 hours
30 g/1 oz dulse, rinsed
1 red onion, diced
1 tbsp miso
250 ml/8 fl oz water

Make sure you've soaked your oats in advance. Rinse the dulse, and dice the onion. Put everything in the blender, and puree until you have a thick batter. On dehydrator sheets, spread the batter into thin cracker shapes around 8-10 cm (3-4 inch) in diameter, and dehydrate for about 8 hours. Flip, and dry on the other side for a further 4 hours until crispy. Store in an airtight container; it will keep for at least a few weeks.

Dulse contains fifteen times more calcium, weight for weight, than cow's milk.

Makes about 25 crackers
Takes 20 minutes, with 4 hours pre-soaking, plus 12 hours dehydrating time
You need a blender and a dehydrator

HUMMUS CRACKERS

We eat a lot of hummus, it's a wonderful source of vegetarian protein, so I hit upon the idea of dehydrating it into crackers so we could enjoy it even more often. It's also a good way to use up leftover hummus before it starts going off.

Hummus (page 41)
2 carrots
1 stick celery
2 tbsp parsley
125 ml/4 fl oz water

Prepare the hummus according to the recipe on page 41. Prepare your carrots and celery for the blender or food processor. Put everything in the machine, and puree until you have a thick batter. On dehydrator trays, spread the batter into thin crackers around 8-10 cm (3-4 inch) in diameter, and dehydrate for about 8 hours. Flip and dry for another 4 hours on the other side, until crunchy. Store in an airtight container, keeps well for a good few weeks.

Hummus is a wonderful source of calcium. If you are trying to cut back on dairy produce but finding it difficult, try increasing the amount of calcium-rich plant foods in your diet; it could be that this is what your body is missing that makes you crave the animal products.

Makes about 25 crackers // Takes 30 minutes, plus 12 hours dehydrating
You need a blender and a dehydrator

RAW-VITA

Before I got my dehydrator, I often used to supplement my salad with crackers
and rice cakes. It was so gratifying to be able to make my own raw versions, just as
pleasantly filling. These are a worthwhile base for any topping, sweet or savoury.

150 g/5 oz rye, soaked 10-12
  hours, sprouted 3 days
60 g/2 oz flaxseed, ground
1 tbsp tamari
250ml/8 fl oz water

Makes about 20 large crackers
Takes 20 minutes to make,
  with time to sprout the rye,
  plus 12 hours dehydrating
You need a blender and a dehydrator

Make sure you've sprouted your rye grains in advance.
Put everything in the blender, and puree until you have
a thick batter. On dehydrator trays, spread the batter into
thin, large, rectangular crackers, about 14 cm (5½ inch) x 7
cm (3 inch) and dehydrate for about 8 hours. Flip and dry
on the other side for a further 4 hours until crispy. Store
in an airtight container – keeps well for at least a month.
    Rye reputedly helps with weight loss, hence its use in
the slimming cracker.

TOMATO CRISPS

Dried tomatoes possess an incredibly intense sweetness which add depth to a dish.
In this recipe, they make delightful crisps that are a wonderful alternative to
potato crisps, and go well with dips such as hummus and guacamole.
For a decent sized bag of crisps, multiply the recipe by three.

5 tomatoes

Serves 1
Takes 5 minutes, plus 18 hours
  dehydrating time
You need a blender and a dehydrator

Put tomatoes in food processor and puree until they
are a soupy mixture, with no lumps left. Carefully pour
onto a dehydrator tray, spreading as thinly as possible.
Dehydrate for twelve to eighteen hours, until completely
dry and crisp. The length of time varies greatly between
different varieties of tomato – the more watery the
tomato, the longer it will take. Fleshier tomatoes work
better and have more flavour. When done, remove the
sheet, and snap into crisp-sized pieces. Store in a sealed
plastic bag for your very own packet of raw crisps.
    These are addictive – like a certain brand of crisp that
comes in a tube, once you start, you can't stop! Experiment
with different flavours: I particularly like a tablespoon of
nori flakes added to the blended tomatoes, but all herbs
and spices work well, or try a teaspoon of tamari and a
tablespoon of apple cider vinegar.

KALE CHIPS

If you have never tried kale chips, you are in for a treat. Every raw fooders' favourite snack (after raw chocolate). Apparently Gwyneth Paltrow makes hers in the oven so even if you haven't got a dehydrator you can give it a go.

500 g/1lb kale
125 g/4 oz sunflower seeds
125 ml/4 fl oz olive oil
½ tsp rock salt
1 fresh date
¼ red onion
1 clove garlic
juice 1 lemon
125 ml/4 fl oz water

Serves 4
Takes 10 minutes, with 2-4 hours pre-soaking and 18 hours dehydrating
You need a blender and ideally a dehydrator

Pre-soak the sunflower seeds for at least two hours. When they are ready, tear the kale into pieces ready for the dehydrator. Remove any excess stalks as these go woody and indigestible when they are dried. There is no need to worry about breaking the kale leaves into tiny pieces. I like them as big leaves, plus if you want to break them down it's much easier to do it once they are dried and crispy.

To make the sauce, drain the seeds and put them in the blender with all the other ingredients: olive oil, salt, a date, red onion, garlic, lemon juice and water. Blend for a minute until creamy. Don't worry if it tastes too oniony at this stage; the onions will change flavour in the dehydrator and, along with the sunflower seeds, imbue the kale chips with their irresistible flavour. Pour the mixture over the kale, and mix thoroughly, so the kale is evenly coated. Spread over three or four dehydrator trays and dry for eighteen hours. After about twelve hours it's good to turn them and check that some aren't still a bit soggy; it tends to be that while most are drying, some get clumped together or have more dressing on, so you want to separate these ones out so they dry properly.

I have been making kale (or spinach or chard or greens) chips more or less every week for a few years now, and I still have to tell you, I have no idea how long they keep because they have never been known to last more than a couple of hours in our house.

'ROASTED' NUTS

These are a staple in our house. A big reason to invest in a dehydrator. We eat them as snacks, sprinkle them on salads, or add them to savoury dishes where nuts are required, for extra flavour. They take on the salty, crunchy qualities of roasted nuts without the unhealthy effects of refined salt and heated oils.

250 g/8 oz walnuts
250 g/8 oz cashews
125 g/4 oz sunflower seeds
125 g/4 oz pumpkin seeds
600 ml/1 pint shoyu (or tamari)

Makes about 25 servings
Takes 10 minutes, with 20 hours
marinating and soaking time
in advance, and 12-24 hours
dehydrating time
You need a dehydrator

Put the nuts and seeds in a large bowl or bucket, and soak for 8 hours in pure water. At the end of this time, drain off the water, and marinate in shoyu for 12 hours. When done, drain off the shoyu, and dehydrate for up to 24 hours. They keep indefinitely, stored in airtight containers.

The shoyu can be reused 2-3 times for marinating. It may develop harmless white yeasts, which you should remove. If it starts to smell, throw it away! You can also add your favourite herbs and spices to the marinade, but this will probably mean it's not reusable.

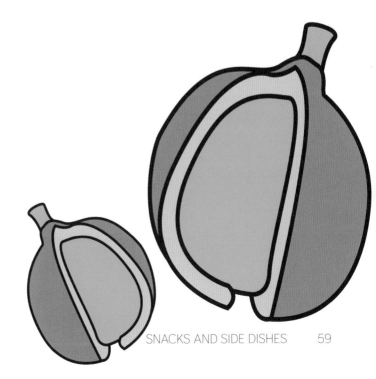

SPRING ROLLS

You can grow your own mung bean sprouts, or buy standard supermarket beansprouts. These are specially grown to make them long and straight, and bear little outward similarity to homegrown sprouts. Homegrown ones are way more nutritious, while shop-bought ones make a more authentic dish.

1 clove garlic

small bunch coriander

1 cm/½ inch piece fresh ginger

¼ red onion

90 g/3 oz cabbage

1 carrot

½ red pepper

90 g/3 oz mung bean sprouts (see page 18)

1 tbsp tamari

1 tbsp rice vinegar

1 tbsp agave syrup

2 tbsp sesame oil

6 large Romaine (Cos) lettuce leaves

In the food processor or blender, mash the garlic, parsley, ginger and onion. Next, grate the cabbage, carrot and red pepper. Transfer everything (apart from the lettuce leaves) to a mixing bowl, and stir thoroughly, until evenly mixed. When the filling is ready, take the lettuce leaves, spread them out on a plate, and dollop a few spoons of the filling on each leaf, making sure you divide it evenly between the leaves. With a knife or the back of a spoon, spread the filling across the leaf, covering it all. Finally, roll the leaf tightly from top to bottom (but not too tightly or the filling will splurge out the sides!). These will taste even better the next day, once the flavours have started to marinade.

Serves 6 // Takes 30 minutes
You need a food processor or blender

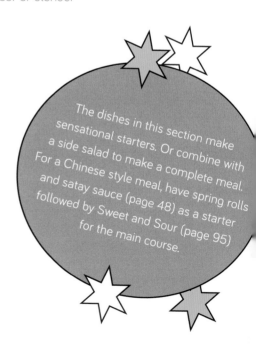

The dishes in this section make sensational starters. Or combine with a side salad to make a complete meal. For a Chinese style meal, have spring rolls and satay sauce (page 48) as a starter followed by Sweet and Sour (page 95) for the main course.

STUFFED MUSHROOMS

If, like me, you love olives, this is an excuse to eat lots of them!
Olives and mushrooms are a gorgeous earthy combination.
The most amazing olives I've ever had are the black Botija olives you find in the USA.

200 g/6½ oz pitted black olives
30 g/1 oz sun-dried tomatoes, pre-
   soaked
2 carrots, chopped
1 stick celery, chopped
2 tbsp fresh parsley
2 tbsp fresh basil
1 clove garlic
2 tbsp flaxseed, ground
2 tbsp tahini
2 portobello (flat) mushrooms

Make sure you've pre-ground your flaxseeds. If you can soak your sun-dried tomatoes in water for about an hour before you start, that will help soften them so they break down in the food processor nicely. Prepare your carrots, celery and herbs for the machine. Put everything apart from the mushrooms in the food processor, and process down to a smooth puree. Cover the underside of the mushrooms with this mixture. If you are able, dehydrate for about four hours before serving.

Olives have the highest mineral count of any fruit, and are also abundant in amino acids, essential fatty acids, and antioxidants.

Serves 2 // Takes 20 minutes
You need a food processor

'CHEESY' STUFFED PEPPERS

I adore stuffed peppers – almost any combination of nuts and vegetables tastes fantastic in that crispy red or yellow shell. However, this has got to be the best filling I've made, it's unbelievably cheesy!

375 g/13 oz corn kernels
2 carrots, chopped
small bunch parsley, chopped
2 tbsp ground flaxseed
2 tbsp extra virgin olive oil
1 tsp miso
2 tbsp nutritional yeast flakes
½ red chilli pepper
2 cloves garlic
125 ml/4 fl oz orange juice
2 large red peppers

Serves 2-4 // Takes 30 minutes
You need a blender

Make sure you've chopped your carrots and parsley in preparation. Also check you've got your ground flaxseeds. Put everything apart from the peppers and orange juice in the blender. Puree, adding orange juice gradually until the mixture turns over. Don't use all the juice if you don't have to, you want the mixture to be as thick as possible, but without lumps. Next, slice the peppers in half lengthways and remove the stalk and seeds. Then fill the peppers with the cheese mixture. If possible, dehydrate for six hours.

One ear of corn has approximately 800 kernels arranged in 16 rows. Fresh corn on the cob makes a great raw snack – juicy and refreshing, just eat it as it is. We put them in the dehydrator for an hour or so to warm them, then brush them with olive oil, and sprinkle rock salt and black pepper over them.

DILL STUFFED PEPPERS

If you prefer, you can also make this using pumpkin seeds instead of sunflower seeds. Use 60 g/2 oz of pumpkin seeds, and soak them overnight first. Pumpkin seeds are a very good source of zinc. (Picture opposite)

60 g/2 oz sprouted sunflower
  seeds
2 tbsp tahini
1 carrot, chopped
1 stick celery, chopped
¼ red onion
small bunch dill
1 tsp tamari
1 lemon, juiced
3 red peppers

Put the sprouted sunflower seeds, tahini, carrot, celery, onion, and dill in the food processor, and process until they are thoroughly blended. Add the tamari and lemon juice, and mix again so you have a thick puree. I think it's nicer if you don't try and get it completely smooth, but leave some texture. Next, slice the peppers in half lengthways and remove the stalk and seeds. Then stuff the peppers with the sunflower mixture and if possible, dehydrate for four hours.

Red peppers are sweeter and more flavourful than their green counterparts, as well as containing nine times more vitamin A, and twice as much vitamin C. Green peppers are not ripened, and much harder to digest.

Serves 3-6 // Takes 30 minutes, make sure you've sprouted your sunflower seeds in advance
You need a food processor

STUFFED AVOCADO

Perfect as a starter. 'Roasted' seeds (page 59) work well in this dish, or Raw Living Sunseeds.

60 g/2 oz sunflower and/or
   pumpkin seeds, pre-soaked
1 carrot, chopped
2 tbsp sun-dried tomatoes
1 tsp miso
½ red onion
¼ red chilli pepper
15 g/½ oz fresh basil leaves
30 g/1 oz alfalfa sprouts
2 avocados

Serves 2 as a main dish,
or 4 as a side dish
Takes 30 minutes, plus
2-4 hours pre-soaking
You need a food processor

Pre-soak your seeds 2-4 hours. If you soak your sun-dried tomatoes for an hour in advance, it will soften them, and help them break down easier in the food processor. Prepare your carrots and onion. Put everything apart from the alfalfa and avocados in the food processor and process until you have a thick puree. Next, slice the avocados in half and remove the stones. Then fill the holes where the stones were with the mixture, and cover the flesh with a thin layer. Top with alfalfa sprouts, to cover each half, and serve on a bed of lettuce.

I love avocados just as they are: I simply half them, remove the stone, sprinkle with a little rock salt and scoop out the flesh from the shell with a spoon; for some reason, when eaten this way I find them reminiscent of boiled eggs.

FALAFEL

Falafel is a Middle Eastern dish, traditionally served with salad and hummus in pitta bread. These taste divine on their own, or try using lettuce or Chinese leaves for the pitta, and fill with raw hummus (page 41), alfalfa, lettuce and tomato for a complete meal.

250 g/8 oz chick peas, sprouted
   (see page 18) or walnuts
   (soaked)
2 tbsp tahini
125 ml/4 fl oz extra virgin olive
   oil
1 tsp tamari
125 ml/4 fl oz lemon juice
bunch fresh coriander
2 cloves garlic
¼ red onion
2 tsp ground cumin
1 tsp honey

If you're using walnuts, soak them for at least 4 hours before you start. If you're using chick peas, make sure you've sprouted them in advance. Put everything in the blender, and puree for a few minutes until the mixture is a smooth batter. Place tablespoons of the mixture onto a dehydrating sheet, about 2 cm (1 inch) high. Dehydrate for about 18 hours.

These are tricky to make without a dehydrator. You can try making them in the food processor instead. Use less extra virgin olive oil, tamari and lemon juice, so the mixture is less liquid and sticks together more. Then roll them into balls by hand.

Makes about 20 // Takes 30 minutes, with time to either pre-soak the walnuts or sprout the chick peas in advance, plus 18 hours drying // You need a blender and a dehydrator

ONION BHAJIS

You can use any vegetable in place of the onion – try broccoli, cauliflower, spinach or pea bhajis. Or double the quantities and make mixed veg bhajis.

30-60 g/1-2 oz onion, diced
250 g/8 oz chick pea sprouts (see page 18) or soaked walnuts
2 tbsp extra virgin olive oil
1 tbsp tamari
2 tbsp water
½ red chilli pepper
½ tsp ground cumin
1 clove garlic
1 tbsp garam masala

Finely chop the onion, or whichever vegetable you are using. Put all the other ingredients in the blender and puree until you have a smooth batter. Stir in the onion (or diced vegetables) with a spoon. Form into patty shapes about 2 cm (1 inch) high, and dehydrate for about 10 hours.

Like the falafel, I feel that these are superior to their cooked counterparts – not so fatty and starchy, but still bursting with exotic flavour.

Makes 10 // Takes 30 minutes, with time to pre-soak your walnuts or sprout your chickpeas, plus 10 hours drying time // You need a blender and a dehydrator

CURRIED SPINACH

One of my favourite Indian dishes was Sag Aloo, which is curried spinach and potatoes. This is my raw version – I used to sometimes add a few chopped boiled potatoes to make it more authentic, and it would really hit the spot.

125 g/4 oz spinach or chard
1 tsp miso
1 tsp tahini
1 tsp garam masala
¼ red onion, diced
¼ red chilli pepper, finely chopped

Break down spinach in a food processor for a couple of minutes, until it is a thick paste. Add the remaining ingredients and process briefly until they are blended in.

Serve with Spicy Carrot and Apple Salad (page 71) and Onion Bhajis (see recipe above) for a complete Indian meal.

Serves 1 // Takes 10 minutes // You need a food processor

MARINATED MUSHROOMS

Crimini mushrooms are very small button mushrooms. If you can't get them,
use chestnut mushrooms and slice about ½ cm/¼ inch thick.

125 ml/4 fl oz extra virgin olive oil
4 tbsp tamari
200 g/6½ oz crimini mushrooms
4 cloves garlic, crushed

Serves 2
Takes 10 minutes, with 8-12 hours
marinating time
You don't need any special
equipment

Put the mushrooms and garlic in a large bowl, and pour the olive oil and mushrooms over them. Keep in the fridge for eight to twelve hours, stirring intermittently. At the end of this time, drain and serve.

You can keep these in the fridge, and add a few to salads when you fancy. They make a lovely alternative to fried mushrooms. Be careful to drain off all the excess marinade, so that they're not too greasy. You can save the marinade and reuse it in a salad dressing.

'COOKED' BUCKWHEAT

Gratifying in the winter when you fancy something hot. You can try this with
any sprout, quinoa also works well. I like to heat my water to 80°C, rather than boiling it.
You can easily find temperature controlled kettles that do that for you,
or just get into the habit of turning the kettle off before it boils.

125 g/4 oz sprouted buckwheat
(see page 18)
600 ml/1 pint heated water

Serves 1
Takes 5 minutes to make, and a day
to marinade
You need a thermos flask

Place buckwheat and water in a thermos flask, and screw the lid on. Leave for twenty-four hours. When done, spoon out of the flask, and serve with gravy (page 49). Eat it immediately, and it will still taste warm and cooked.

You can turn this into a complete meal by adding grated vegetables such as carrot, chopped herbs, and seasonings such as miso and garlic to the thermos.

Side Salads

SWEET APPLE SALAD

SPICY CARROT AND
APPLE SALAD

APPLE AND OLIVE
SALAD

THE BEST
COLESLAW

EAT YOUR GREENS

SWEET GREENS

PAD THAI

CELERIAC SALAD

CREAMY BEETROOT SALAD

CARROT CAKE SALAD

CAULIFLOWER CHEESE

LENTIL AND
WATERCRESS SALAD

CHRIS'S LUNCH

CUCUMBERS AND KETCHUP

MISO MUSHROOMS

PESTO SALAD

Main Course
Salads

START YOU
OFF SALAD

SAUERKRAUT
SALAD

ALMOND, AVOCADO AND
MUSHROOM SALAD

THAI GREEN PAPAYA SALAD

CHRIS'S SALAD

SWEET APPLE SALAD

A sweet salad. Serve as a snack, or as an accompaniment to spicy dishes.

2 apples, grated
2 tbsp raisins
2 tbsp dates
2 tbsp coconut flakes
1 tbsp almond butter
1 tbsp yacon syrup
½ tsp Chinese 5-spice

Grate the apples. Chop the dates up into small pieces. In a bowl with a spoon, mix the yacon syrup, almond butter and Chinese 5-spice. Toss all the ingredients together and serve immediately.

I always use fresh coconut, or coconut flakes. Desiccated is an acceptable alternative, although it isn't raw. If you prefer, you can use raw honey instead of yacon syrup.

Serves 2 // Takes 15 minutes // You need a grater

SPICY CARROT AND APPLE SALAD

This salad is an interesting mix of sweet, spicy and sour. Bombay mix obviously isn't raw: if you want this salad to be fully raw, choose one of the interesting activated nut ranges on the market instead, there are many amazing flavours to choose from, such as our own Raw Living Sunseeds.

250 g/8 oz carrot, grated
250 g/8 oz apple, grated
1 tbsp flaxseed oil
1 tbsp Bombay mix
1 tbsp Indian pickle

Grate the carrot and apple. Toss all ingredients together, and serve immediately or the Bombay mix will go soft.

You can buy Indian pickle from supermarkets, or an Asian grocer. It comes in many different varieties, the two most popular being mango and lime. It is not raw, but adds wonderful flavour and authenticity to your Indian dishes.

Serves 2 // Takes 15 minutes // You need a grater

APPLE AND OLIVE SALAD

As olives are a fruit, they combine surprisingly well with apples. You can also try substituting apples for oranges in this recipe: use 2 oranges, peeled and chopped.

125 g/4 oz apple, grated
3 lettuce leaves, shredded
100g/ 3½ oz olives
1 tbsp flaxseed oil
1 tsp liquid Aminos

Grate the apple, and shred the lettuce. Toss all ingredients together and serve.

It is difficult to be sure that you are buying raw olives. Canned ones are pasteurised, and are best avoided. Pitted olives have nearly always been heat-treated. The best ones to buy are sun-ripened black olives, if you can find them. In the UK, there are a few companies who guarantee their olives are raw, such as Olives et Al and Raw Health.

Serves 2 // Takes 15 minutes to make // You need a grater

THE BEST COLESLAW

This is a basic coleslaw recipe so feel free to experiment with it. For example, you could use red cabbage, or replace the carrot with beetroot or apple. Also I am a big fan of fermented vegetables, and love to substitute some of the cabbage in this recipe with sauerkraut. The amount of mayonnaise you use will depend on its viscosity – thicker mayonnaise will coat the vegetables better. You can find a raw mayo recipe on page 47, or you could use vegan soya mayonnaise or organic egg mayonnaise.

2 carrots
200 g /6½ oz white cabbage
½ red onion
1 tbsp whole hemp seeds
2 tbsp mayonnaise
freshly ground sea salt and black
    pepper

Grate carrot, cabbage and onion then toss with remaining ingredients. Add salt and pepper to taste.

   We use hemp seeds as they add a lovely crunch to this dish, but you could use pine nuts, sesame seeds, or walnuts.

Serves 2 // Takes 15 minutes to make
You need a grater

EAT YOUR GREENS

When I wrote the original edition of this book, this was one of my favourite recipes in it; I used to make it all the time. It comes out quite differently, depending on which greens you use. Spinach and lettuce are quite runny, kale is quite chewy. Experiment with different combinations to see which you like best.

100-200 g/3-7 oz green leafy
    vegetables
½ avocado
2 gherkins (or 2 tbsp sauerkraut)
1 tbsp dulse
1 tsp kelp powder

Put greens in food processor and process until they are evenly chopped with no large pieces remaining. Add avocado and process for half a minute, until it is completely mixed with the greens. Then add the remaining ingredients and process briefly until they are mixed in. The resulting mix should not be a puree, but still have some texture, with the individual ingredients discernible. Serve as a side salad to burgers (page 88-89) or nut loaf (page 85).

   I've used spinach, kale, cavalo nero, chard, green cabbage, pak choi, chinese leaf, lettuce, and celery in this dish. It also provides a welcome use for leftover broccoli stems.

Serves 1
Takes 10 minutes
You need a food processor

SWEET GREENS

This is another unusual combination that is surprisingly tasty. Serve as an accompaniment to Onion Bhajis (page 68) and Spicy Carrot and Apple Salad (page 71).

100-200 g/3-7 oz greens (see previous recipe)
½ avocado
2 tbsp fresh tamarind or date paste
1 tbsp dulse
1 tbsp garam masala

Put the greens in the food processor and break down to a mash. Add remaining ingredients and process for a minute until they are blended in.

Fresh tamarind is hard to come across, but worth getting if you can. It has a similar taste to dates, and is a common ingredient in Indian chutneys and curries. If you can't find it, use dates instead.

Serves 1 // Takes 10 minutes // You need a food processor

PAD THAI

My raw version of the classic Thai noodle dish. Kelp noodles are an extremely popular raw packaged food made from the sea vegetable kelp, and nothing else. If you can't get kelp noodles, grated daikon, courgette, green papaya, jerusalem artichokes, or even, at a push, white cabbage, would do. If you have a Spiralizer, you could use spiralized courgette. Regarding the sesame oil, toasted has a more authentic and stronger flavour, but is obviously not raw.

1 packet kelp noodles
1 tbsp sesame oil
1 tbsp agave syrup
1 tbsp tamari
2 cloves garlic, crushed
1 red chilli pepper, finely chopped
2 lettuce leaves
2 Chinese cabbage
6 cherry tomatoes
2 mushrooms, sliced
45 g/1½ oz green beans, chopped
45 g/1½ oz mung bean sprouts (see page 18)
2 tbsp cashews, chopped

You need to start by preparing the kelp noodles. Cut open the packet, rinse them well, and marinade them in a medium-sized bowl in the sesame oil, agave, tamari, garlic and chilli. The longer you leave them marinading the better they taste: up to four hours is good. Finely slice the mushrooms and green beans, and add them to the bowl of kelp noodles. Add the bean sprouts as welltt. Shred the lettuce and Chinese cabbage into small pieces. Halve the cherry tomatoes. Using salad servers, mix the lettuce, Chinese leaf and tomatoes together. Arrange on a plate as a bed for the rest of the salad. When the kelp noodles have finished marinading (or you can't wait any longer!) place the noodle mixture on the lettuce bed, and sprinkle the chopped cashews over the top.

Kelp noodles, like tofu, have no flavour straight out of the packet and aren't very appetising. But marinade them for a while and they absorb the flavours of the marinade and become much softer. They are a popular way to consume sea vegetables because they don't have any of that seaweed flavour that some people find off-putting.

Serves 2
Takes 20 minutes to make. If you can marinade the kelp noodles at least 4 hours in advance, that will improve the flavour of the dish considerably
You don't need any special equipment

CELERIAC SALAD

Shredded celeriac in a spicy mayonnaise sauce is a traditional Northern European dish. Celeriac is like the root of the celery plant. It has a strong, interesting flavour, not like any other vegetable.

½ celeriac
2 tbsp Almond Mayo (page 47)
1 tsp cayenne pepper

Serves 2 // Takes 10 minutes, best marinated at least 12 hours
You need a grater

Peel and grate the celeriac. Toss all the ingredients together, and marinate in fridge for 12-24 hours, to soften the celeriac.

Celeriac is an underused English vegetable – if you're cooking, it's particularly appetizing when made into chips (see page 156). It also goes well with Umeboshi Dressing on page 46.

CREAMY BEETROOT SALAD

Choose smaller beetroots, which are sweeter than the larger ones.
The leaves are mineral rich, and also edible; use like spinach.

250 g/8 oz beetroot
250 g/8 oz apple
2 tbsp mayonnaise
1 tbsp shelled hemp seeds

Serves 2 // Takes 15 minutes
You need a grater

Peel and grate the beetroot. Grate the apple. Use any kind of mayo that you favour: organic egg mayonnaise, soyannaise, or one of the raw recipes in this book. Toss all ingredients together and serve.

Apples are one of the most popular fruits in the world, growing almost everywhere: there are around 40 million tons of apples produced every year. There are over three thousand varieties.

CARROT CAKE SALAD

This is a very sweet salad, which is best served on its own, as a snack, or as an accompaniment to a green salad. It's a great one to serve children.

1 tbsp tahini
1 tbsp agave syrup
1 tsp cinnamon
water to mix
3 carrots
2 tbsp raisins
2 tbsp goji berries
90 g/3 oz wheat sprouts (see page 18)

In a small bowl, mix the tahini, agave syrup, cinnamon and a little water to make a thick dressing. Next, grate the carrots. Put them in a large bowl with the raisins, gojis and wheat sprouts. Pour the dressing over, and give it all a good toss.

Carrots are one of the best sources of carotene, which the body converts to vitamin A and the second most popular vegetable in the world after the potato.

Serves 2 // Takes 15 minutes // You need a grater

CAULIFLOWER CHEESE

If you want to impress guests, multiply this recipe by four, and use a whole intact cauliflower. If you have a dehydrator, this is wonderful warmed through for a few hours before serving. Mark Twain famously claimed that cauliflower is 'nothing but a cabbage with a college education'.

300 g/10 oz cauliflower, divided
   into bite-sized florets
125 g/4 oz tahini
1 tsp tamari
1 lemon, juiced
2 tbsp water
2 tbsp nutritional yeast flakes

Put all the ingredients except the cauliflower in a bowl and blend together with a hand whisk. Pour over cauliflower, toss and serve.

As an alternative to cauliflower, try purple cauliflower, romanesco, which is a green cauliflower with beautiful spiralling florets, broccoli, or purple sprouting broccoli.

Serves 2 // Takes 10 minutes
You don't need any special equipment

LENTIL AND WATERCRESS SALAD

Watercress is so health giving – packed full of minerals, particularly iron and calcium, as well as being rich in vitamins A and C. I recommend using unpasteurised goats' or sheeps' yoghurt, or live soya yoghurt in this recipe.

1 bunch watercress
60 g/2 oz lentil sprouts (see page
   18)
½ avocado, diced
½ tsp Seagreens
1 tbsp plain live yoghurt

Using scissors, cut and discard the stems of the watercress, and snip the rest into bite-sized pieces. Then put all ingredients in a bowl and toss together.

Watercress is a native English herb. It doesn't keep well, so use on the day of purchase. If you need to keep it, store with the stems in a glass of water, and a plastic bag over the leaves; all cut herbs are best stored this way.

Serves 2 // Takes 10 minutes
You don't need any special equipment

CHRIS'S LUNCH

A simple favourite of ours when we were first raw. It makes a quick, scrumptious, satisfying lunch. If you want the recipe to be fully raw, replace the Bombay mix with some activated spicy nuts such as Gone Nuts or Raw Living Sunseeds.

1 avocado
3 tomatoes
2 tbsp Bombay mix
½ tbsp liquid aminos
freshly ground black
  pepper

Cube avocado and tomatoes. Toss all ingredients together. Add pepper to taste.

Serves 2 // Takes 5 minutes
You don't need any special equipment

CUCUMBERS AND KETCHUP

I don't think this would be quite the same with traditional ketchup!

½ cucumber
1 red pepper
2 tbsp fresh dill
2 tbsp tomato ketchup
  (see recipe page 45)

Dice the cucumber. Remove the seeds and stem from the pepper and dice that as well. Chop the dill into as tiny pieces as you can. Toss all ingredients together.

This is a popular salad with children – don't they love anything that's covered in ketchup?

Serves 2 // Takes 10 minutes // You don't need any special equipment

MISO MUSHROOMS

This has a rich decadent flavour. Shiitake mushrooms are also consumed for their medicinal benefits, as they contain unique polysaccharides which are exceptionally immune boosting.

1 tbsp miso
2 tbsp tahini
2 tbsp water
1 tbsp apple cider vinegar
1 clove garlic, minced
200 g/6½ oz oyster or shiitake mushrooms

Using a hand whisk beat together all the ingredients apart from the mushrooms. Then slice the mushrooms into small pieces, and toss in the sauce. If you have time, leave it to marinate for a few hours before eating.

If you can't get speciality mushrooms, chestnut mushrooms work just as well. As oyster mushrooms have a fairly robust flavour when eaten raw, you may want to mix half and half.

Serves 2 // Takes 10 minutes (if you have time, marinade for a few hours before eating) // You don't need any special equipment

PESTO SALAD

Pesto, the Italian basil dressing is traditionally made with cheese and added to pasta. You can make your own raw vegan pesto (there is a recipe in my book *Raw Living*), or you can purchase vegan pesto from a whole food store, and use it as salad dressing. I love Seggiano pesto, which is made from pine nuts and cashews and is also raw.

3 mushrooms
3 tomatoes
1 avocado
2 tbsp pesto
1 tbsp nutritional yeast flakes
1 tbsp pine nuts
2 tsp nori flakes

Fine slice the mushrooms. Dice the tomatoes and avocado. Place in a bowl and toss with the remaining ingredients.

Choose chestnut mushrooms that have tightly closed caps; if the gills are showing, it means they are past their best.

Serves 2
Takes 10 minutes
You don't need any special equipment

START YOU OFF SALAD

This is my foolproof recipe for an unbeatable main course salad
that can be adapted to whatever you have around the kitchen.

200 g/6½ oz leafy greens
300 g/10 oz non-sweet fruit
150 g/5 oz vegetables
30 g/1 oz alfalfa sprouts (see page 18)
60 g/2 oz bean sprouts
sea vegetables
2 tbsp fermented vegetables
1 avocado
2 tbsp crunchy bits
dressing

Serves 2-4
Takes 20 minutes
You don't need any special equipment

Don't forget about the many different varieties of lettuce available – for example, cos (also known as Romaine), iceberg, butterhead, oak leaf, lollo rosso, frisee, little gem, radicchio, endive.

Start with two types of leafy greens, such as lettuce, baby leaf spinach, watercress, pak choi, Chinese leaf, lambs leaf, kale, rocket, purslane, mizuna. Use 100 g /3 oz of each. Don't rinse, and don't use a knife on them, as this makes them lose their crispness. If they need cleaning, wipe them with a kitchen towel. If you are using organic leaves don't be so fastidious – a bit of organic soil is good for you! Make sure that you check carefully for bugs. Tear greens into small pieces; watercress may need chopping with scissors, leave small leaves such as lambs leaf whole.

Add two types of non-sweet fruit (150 g/5 oz of each), for example, tomatoes, cucumber, pepper, or mushroom. Then add a vegetable; our favourites are broccoli, cauliflower, celery, grated carrot, or grated beetroot. Put in some alfalfa sprouts, and more sprouts such as lentil, mung bean, or sunflower. Next add seaweed – 2 tbsp dulse, arame, or hijiki, 1 tbsp nori flakes, or 1 nori sheet cut into small pieces. Then you want some sour vegetables like gherkins, sauerkraut, or kimchi, and don't forget one avocado, cubed. Finally, add crunchy bits such as activated nuts or seeds, or Bombay mix. Toss all ingredients together with salad servers.

Dress and serve immediately (see dressings pages 45-46). If you make a salad and leave it to stand, it will go limp and soggy. If you have to make it in advance, prepare all the ingredients and leave dressing it until the very last minute.

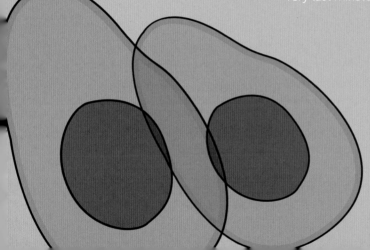
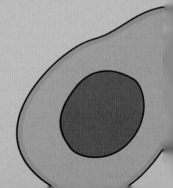

SAUERKRAUT SALAD

Sauerkraut is cabbage that has been grated and allowed to ferment. A traditional German dish, it is full of enzymes and beneficial bacteria, and wonderful for the digestion. Most sauerkraut you buy in the stores won't be raw, but there are some specific unpasteurised brands around. My favourite is Cultured Probiotics.

200 g/6½ oz lettuce leaves
200 g/6½ oz spinach leaves
1 avocado
3 tomatoes
30 g/1 oz dulse, rinsed
250 g/8 oz sauerkraut
30 g/1 oz alfalfa sprouts (see page 18)
1 tsp kelp powder
1 tsp liquid aminos
1 tbsp hemp oil

Wash and tear the lettuce and spinach leaves. Dice the avocado and tomatoes. Rinse the dulse. Put all the ingredients in a large bowl, and toss until evenly mixed.

Lettuce contains a very mild opiate, which is why a large green salad leaves you feeling so calm and relaxed. Wild lettuce, which is usually sold dried, like a herb, can be smoked for its sedative effect.

Serves 2 // Takes 15 minutes
You don't need any special equipment

ALMOND, AVOCADO AND MUSHROOM SALAD

This is a hearty, high protein salad.

200 g/6½ oz lettuce
1 bunch watercress
½ avocado
2 tbsp dulse, rinsed and torn
100 g/ 3½ oz brown mushrooms
125 g/4 oz soaked almonds or cubed tofu
30 g/1 oz alfalfa sprouts (see page 18)
60 g/2 oz cherry tomatoes, halved
2 tbsp olives, pitted

Serves 2 // Takes 15 minutes
You don't need any special equipment

Rinse and tear the lettuce and put it in a large salad bowl. Chop the watercress, discarding any woody stems, and add that in. Cube the avocado and pop it in. Rinse the dulse, tear it, and add it into the salad. Fine slice the mushrooms. Toss everything together. Serve with a thick creamy dressing such as Ultimate Dressing (page 45).

Tofu isn't a raw food; it is made from cooked, pressed soyabeans. It is high in protein and calcium, and originates from Japan. Once touted as an essential part of the vegetarian diet, soya is now experiencing something of a backlash because of the oestrogen mimickers it contains. If you prefer to avoid soya, soak some almonds for at least a couple of hours and use them, or buy some of the pre-packaged activated nuts and seeds.

THAI GREEN PAPAYA SALAD

This is one of the most popular Thai salads. You can also substitute green mango for the green papaya. These are simply unripe fruit, in which the starches have not turned to sugars, so they are not sweet.

½ green papaya
45 g/ 1½ oz green beans
2 tbsp mung bean sprouts (see page 18)
2 tbsp chopped cashews

DRESSING
2 tomatoes
2 cloves garlic
1 red chilli pepper
1 tsp tamari
1 tbsp agave syrup
juice ½ lemon

Peel the papaya, remove the seeds, and grate the flesh. Finely slice the green beans. Toss all salad ingredients together. Prepare all your dressing ingredients for the blender – chop the tomatoes, peel the garlic, and de-seed the chilli pepper. Blend the dressing ingredients together until they form a smooth puree – be especially careful not to leave any lumps of garlic or chilli! Toss salad in dressing.

In Thailand, they serve this with a lot more chilli – beware if you order it in a Thai restaurant. If you do overheat, don't try drinking water, as this makes the burning worse. Eat some ice cream or yoghurt – something cold and creamy.

Serves 2 // Takes 15 minutes
You need a blender and a grater

CHRIS'S SALAD

The secret's in the dressing. Toasted sesame oil is not raw, but a few drops add incredible flavour to a dish. And it combines surprisingly well with a traditional English pickle.

200 g/6½ oz mixed leaves e.g. lettuce, lambs leaf, watercress, baby spinach, rocket

½ red pepper

2 mushrooms

2 tomatoes

2 pickled gherkins

3 marinated sun-dried tomatoes

1 small head broccoli

1 tbsp dulse

1 avocado

2 tbsp sprouts (whatever you have to hand, see page 18)

10 pitted olives

2 tbsp pine kernels

2 tbsp alfalfa sprouts (see page 18)

2 tbsp Bombay mix or activated nuts and seeds

½ tsp kelp powder

½ tbsp liquid aminos

1 tbsp sesame oil

1 tbsp pickle

Rinse and prepare the salad leaves. Finely dice the red pepper, mushrooms, tomatoes, gherkins, sun-dried tomatoes, broccoli, dulse, and avocado, small enough so that you can get a variety of ingredients on your fork in one go. In a large bowl, toss everything together so that all the ingredients are evenly distributed. Then add the sprouts, olives, pine kernels, alfalfa, Bombay mix, and kelp powder, and toss again. Next, tear the leaves and add them in. Finally add the liquid aminos, sesame oil and pickle (which is not a raw food), and toss once more. Serve immediately.

Serves 2

Takes 15 minutes

You don't need any special equipment

Main Courses

NUTTIEST LOAF

SUNFLOWER SAUSAGES

ROLL-UPS

BRAZIL NUT BURGERS

MUSHROOM AND
MISO BURGERS

CREAMY CALCIUM
VEGETABLES

DOLMADES

SPROUTED TABBOULEH

RAWTATOUILLE

UNBEATABLE PIZZA

CORN SUPREME

SWEET AND SOUR

THAI GREEN CURRY

THAI YELLOW CURRY

ALMOND, CAULIFLOWER
AND CHICK PEA CURRY

TOMATO AND
ASPARAGUS CURRY

POTTED KELP
NOODLES

CREAM OF COCONUT
CURRY

NUTTIEST LOAF

This is terrific with Tahini and Miso Gravy (see page 49), Eat Your Greens (page 72), and Cauliflower Cheese (page 77). Unfortunately, there is no adequate raw substitute for roast potatoes to make a traditional Sunday roast!

125 g/4 oz almonds, soaked
125 g/4 oz walnuts, soaked
1 ½ carrots
2 sticks celery
1 red onion
30-60 g/1-2 oz fresh herbs
   e.g. parsley, basil, dill, rosemary,
   thyme
30 g/1 oz sun-dried tomatoes
60 g/2 oz flaxseed, ground
1 tbsp liquid aminos
1 tsp miso

Pre-soak the almonds and walnuts for 4-8 hours. Make sure you've ground your flaxseeds. When the nuts have finished soaking, grind them as finely as possible in the food processor. Next, prepare the carrot, celery, onion, and herbs, and put them in the food processor with the nuts and sun-dried tomatoes, and process until there are no large lumps or pieces left. Then add the flaxseed, liquid aminos and miso, and process once more until smooth. On a dehydrator tray, shape into a loaf shape about 2 cm (1 inch) high and dehydrate for four hours. When done, slice and serve.

To make **nut cutlets**, follow the exact same recipe, but shape into burgers instead.

Serves 8 // Takes 20 minutes with 4-8 hours pre-soaking and 4 hours dehydrating
You need a food processor and a dehydrator

SUNFLOWER SAUSAGES

My sons often have these for dinner – I hope you find that they taste far better than a lot of the processed vegan sausages you find in the shops.

2 carrots
200 g/6½ oz cabbage
125 g/4 oz sunflower seeds,
   soaked
2 tbsp flaxseed, ground
½ red onion
1 tsp tamari

Soak the sunflower seeds for 2-4 hours. Make sure you've ground your flaxseeds. Chop the carrots and cabbage, put all the ingredients in the food processor, and break down to a thick paste. Shape into sausages about 8 cm x 2.5 cm (3 inch x 1 inch) by rolling between the palms of your hands. Dehydrate for four hours.

You can make this mixture into burgers, if you prefer. Pumpkin sausages are marvellous too – just replace the sunflower seeds with ground pumpkin seeds. If you don't have a dehydrator, these work well lightly fried in a pan.

Makes about 10 sausages // Takes 20 minutes with 2-4 hours
pre-soaking and 8 hours dehydrating // You need a food processor and a dehydrator

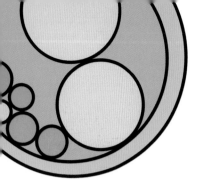

ROLL-UPS

There is no limit to the different combinations of roll-ups you can create. Basically, you take a leaf, spread it with your favourite spread, stuff with some sprouts or vegetables, roll and serve. I make and enjoy these all the time; in fact they were one of things I used to eat when I was raw before I knew I was raw! So I've been eating them for over twenty years without getting bored of them. Here are a few of my favourite combinations.

CARROT: Crazy Carrot Dip (page 38) on lettuce leaves, cover in alfalfa

GUACAMOLE: Guacamole (page 40) on Chinese leaf, cover with alfalfa and mung bean sprouts

RED HOT PEPPER ROLLS: Red Hot Pepper Dip (page 41) on cabbage leaves, cover with lentil sprouts, alfalfa, cucumber and tomato

SPICY: Mayonnaise (page 47) and Indian pickle on lettuce leaves, cover with cucumber, tomato, mushroom and lots of mung bean sprouts

NORI I: Avocado, mushroom, tomato, red chilli, and bean sprouts rolled in a nori sheet

NORI II: Cucumber, tofu (not a raw food), spring onion and alfalfa rolled in a nori sheet

Lettuce leaves work best because they are thin and roll easily. Chinese leaf, pak choi, and large spinach leaves all make respectable rolls. I like white and red cabbage, but they are a bit tougher to chew. Nori sheets are traditionally used in sushi making. If you buy the untoasted variety, they are raw.

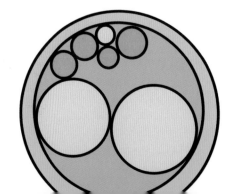

BURGERS

All burgers are fantastic served with a Chinese leaf or lettuce leaf folded round to make a bun, with mayonnaise, ketchup, alfalfa, gherkins, mustard, or whatever your favourite relish is inside. If you have some dehydrated flax crackers you can use that as a 'bun' as well. If you want to go the whole way, serve with coleslaw (page 72), Champion Chips (page 156) and a smoothie (page 151). Or there's a recipe for Courgette Chips in my *Raw Living* book. If you don't have a dehydrator, you can omit the water in the recipe, and then either eat them raw as they are, or grill them lightly on each side; not enough to cook them through but enough to seal them and bring out the flavours.

BRAZIL NUT BURGERS

4 sticks celery
3 carrots
1 red onion
small bunch parsley
250 g/8 oz brazil nuts, soaked
60 g/2 oz flaxseed, ground
2 tbsp nutritional yeast flakes
1 tsp Herbamare

Makes 8 burgers
Takes 15 minutes, with 4-8 hours
pre-soaking
and 12 hours dehydrating
You need a food processor,
and a dehydrator is helpful

Pre-soak your brazils for at least 4 hours. Grind your flaxseeds. Chop the celery, carrots, onion, and parsley so they will fit in the food processor. Put them in the food processor with the nuts, and process until all the ingredients are blended together. Then add the remaining ingredients, and process again to make a thick paste. On a dehydrator tray, shape into burgers about 1 cm/½ inch thick, and dehydrate for eight hours.

Don't attempt to omit the flaxseeds from this recipe, as they are the binding agent. Flaxseeds behave differently from other seeds. You cannot eat them as they are; the easiest way to consume them is by grinding them up and adding them to food. If you soak them for a few hours (not longer), they swell up and form a sticky mass, which resembles frogspawn. You can eat them this way if you choose but they are not very palatable. We most often then dehydrate them and turn them into crackers.

MUSHROOM AND MISO BURGERS

Mushrooms contain protein, minerals and B vitamins, and are rich in polysaccharides, which boost the immune system. Medicinal mushrooms such as chaga and cordyceps are very popular among raw fooders because of their exceptional immune benefits.

2 sticks celery
8 brown mushrooms
1 red onion
150 g/5 oz sesame seeds, soaked
60 g/2 oz flaxseed, ground
1 tbsp miso
2 tsp medicinal mushroom extract (optional)
4 tbsp water

Soak your sesame seeds in advance. Grind your flaxseeds. Prepare the celery, mushroom and onion for the food processor, and then process until they're completely mixed together. Then add the sesame seeds and flaxseeds and process again. Lastly, add miso, water, and medicinal mushroom extract if you are using it, and process once more, until you have a thick paste. On dehydrator trays, shape into burgers about 1 cm/½ inch thick, and dehydrate for eight hours.

Mushrooms are neither a fruit nor a vegetable, but a fungus, in a classification of their own. Both the ancient Chinese and the Romans viewed mushrooms as a food of the gods, and would give them as a divine offering.

Makes 8 burgers // Takes 20 minutes, with 2-4 hours pre-soaking and 8 hours dehydrating
You need a food processor and a dehydrator

CREAMY CALCIUM VEGETABLES

You can also make this recipe with tofu instead of the almonds.
Tofu isn't a raw food but, like almonds, it is very high in calcium.

60 g/2 oz almonds, soaked
½ avocado
1 tbsp nutritional yeast flakes
1 tsp tamari
1 tbsp nori flakes
1 apple, juiced
2 sticks celery, juiced
60 g/2 oz baby spinach leaves
90 g/3 oz broccoli
90 g/3 oz cauliflower
60 g/2 oz lettuce
alfalfa sprouts

Pre-soak your almonds for 4-8 hours. Put all the ingredients in the blender – apart from the broccoli, cauliflower, lettuce and alfalfa – and blend to make a smooth creamy sauce. Then chop the broccoli and cauliflower finely, shred the lettuce, and place in a serving bowl. Pour the sauce over the vegetables and garnish with alfalfa.

A lot of these recipes are far more successful if you have a high power blender (see page 17 for more info). If your blender is not very strong, try adding the liquid ingredients first and then adding the solid ingredients gradually, with the blender running, ensuring that the mixture keeps turning over. If this doesn't work, you can either add a little water (which makes for a sloppier end product), or use the food processor instead, although the result will be more granular in texture.

Serves 2 // Takes 20 minutes, with 4 hours pre-soaking // You need a blender

DOLMADES (STUFFED VINE LEAVES)

This is one of those dishes that I used to love cooked, but tastes even better raw.
If artichokes aren't in season, use cauliflower, white cabbage, celery, or daikon instead.

½ packet vine leaves
500 g/1 lb Jerusalem artichokes
¼ red onion
1 clove garlic
1 tbsp fresh dill
1 tbsp fresh parsley
1 tbsp fresh mint
1 tbsp fresh oregano
½ tsp ground cinnamon
4 tomatoes
juice 1 lemon
2 tbsp extra virgin olive oil
1 tsp tamari
freshly ground pepper

Serves 4
Takes 20 minutes to make,
ideally with at least 2 hours
marinading time
You need a food processor

Firstly, rinse the vine leaves and set aside. Then chop the artichokes in the food processor until the pieces are the same size as rice grains. Remove the artichokes to a bowl, and mix the onions, garlic and tomatoes in the food processor or in a blender, until they're thoroughly broken down. Next put all the ingredients in the bowl with the artichokes, and stir with a spoon so that they're thoroughly mixed. Place a teaspoon or two of this mixture in each vine leaf, rolling each leaf tightly, and pack them closely in a serving dish. Finally, put them in the fridge and leave to marinate for at least a few hours, preferably overnight.

Vine leaves bought in the shops are boiled. If you or someone you know has a grape vine growing in the garden, you pick them fresh off the vine. They have a slightly vinegary taste, and are crispier than the cooked version, but very palatable. Rinse and soak them in pure water for a few hours before use. If you don't have vine leaves you could just use lettuce leaves or nori sheets (just don't tell the Greeks!).

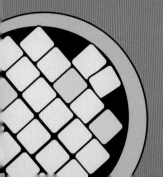

SPROUTED TABBOULEH

Quinoa was a staple of the Incas. It contains the amino acid lysine,
so it provides a more complete protein than other grains. You need to rinse
quinoa before you sprout it, to remove its bitter natural coating.

30 g/1 oz alfalfa sprouts
100 g/3½ oz lettuce, shredded
150 g/5 oz quinoa, sprouted (see
    page 18)
2 tbsp pitted olives
2 tomatoes, chopped
⅓ cucumber, chopped
½ red pepper, chopped
15 g/ ½ oz fresh mint, chopped
small bunch flat leaf parsley,
    chopped
juice ½ lemon
2 tbsp extra virgin olive oil
1 tsp tamari
1 clove garlic, minced

Make sure you've pre-sprouted your quinoa. Fine dice the
tomatoes, cucumber, red pepper, mint and parsley, into as
small as possible pieces. Make a bed for the tabbouleh with
the alfalfa and lettuce. Then toss all the other ingredients
together until they are evenly distributed, and arrange over
the lettuce. If you've got time, leave in the fridge for a few
hours to marinate.

Tabbouleh is a Lebanese salad, traditionally served with
lettuce leaves, which you use to scoop up the tabbouleh to
eat.

Serves 2
Takes 20 minutes, with advance time needed
for sprouting the quinoa
You don't need any special equipment

RAWTATOUILLE

If possible, make this recipe in advance, as the flavours will blend
and the vegetables will soften. It is best 24-48 hours old.

3 mushrooms
1 courgette
1 red pepper
½ portion pasta sauce (page 50)

Slice the vegetables as thinly as possible - use the slicing
blade on your food processor or a mandolin if you
have one. Or you can make courgette ribbons using a
vegetable peeler: peel the courgette from top to bottom,
and keep peeling until you have used as much of the
courgette as you can; finely chop the remainder. Toss the
vegetables in pasta sauce, top with Grated
'Cheese' (page 52) and serve with a
green salad.

A traditional Mediterranean
dish, the original version
contains aubergine which
unfortunately is inedible
raw.

Serves 2
Takes 20 minutes
You don't need any special
equipment, though a mandolin is
useful if you have one.

UNBEATABLE PIZZA

This dish is time-consuming to prepare, but so worth it. Make a batch of bases in advance, and store them in the fridge ready to use. You can't really make the bases without a dehydrator, but you could buy some raw crackers and just make your own raw sauces and toppings.

BASES:

Makes two 20 cm (8 inch) bases

300 g/10 oz buckwheat, sprouted
(see page 18)
1 tbsp tamari
4 tbsp extra virgin olive oil
15 g/ ½ oz fresh basil
30 g/1 oz sun-dried tomatoes
(pre-soaked 1 hour)
½ red onion

Make sure you've sprouted your buckwheat in advance. Put the buckwheat in the food processor or high power blender and process for a couple of minutes until it is completely mashed. Add the basil, tomatoes and onion, and process again so that they are totally amalgamated. Then add the extra virgin olive oil and tamari, and process once more so that you have a smooth batter. Spread two rounds onto dehydrator sheets, about 0.5cm/ ¼ inch thick, and dehydrate for 12 -18 hours.

TOPPING

1 portion Melted 'Cheese'
(page 52)
1 portion Pasta Sauce (page 50)
125-250 g/4-8 oz vegetables (see opposite)
1 portion Grated 'Cheese'
(page 52)

Spread each base with a thin layer of melted cheese, then a thin layer of pasta sauce. Cover with vegetables of your own choice – e.g. thinly sliced mushrooms, pitted and halved olives, sweetcorn kernels, thinly sliced tomato, sunflower sprouts, shredded spinach, broccoli florets, marinated onion, thinly sliced red pepper. Top with Grated 'Cheese'. Eat immediately before it goes soggy.

How densely you cover your pizza is up to you. However if you pile on too much sauce, and layer it with too many toppings, the base is likely to collapse under the weight. These bases are so yummy, it is best not to drown them.

Serves 2 as a main meal or 4 with a side salad
Takes 1 hour. You need to sprout your buckwheat in advance, and allow 12-18 hours for dehydrating
You need a food processor and blender

CORN SUPREME

If you have a Spiralizer, you can use it on the courgettes and carrots and call this pasta! Spiralizers are machines that you turn by hand to make ribbons of vegetables. They sound like the kind of impractical kitchen gadget that you buy and then never use and they sit at the back of the cupboard gathering dust, but actually they are surprisingly simple to use and really do transform your humble vegetables into something far more exciting.

1 carrot
1 courgette
1 cob sweetcorn
60 g/2 oz sunflower sprouts (see page 18)
½ portion pasta sauce (page 50)

Top and tail the carrot. If you have a Spiralizer, you can prepare it in this. If not, using a vegetable peeler, peel it from top to bottom. Keep peeling until you have used as much of the carrot as you can, and made lots of beautiful orange ribbons (finely chop the remainder). Now do the same to the courgette. Because the ribbons are so thin, raw vegetables peeled in this way are very easy to eat, and it makes a welcome change from chopping and grating. Remove the sweetcorn kernels from the cob by holding the cob upright and slicing downwards between the kernels and the core. Hold it over a bowl or a plate or the kernels will spray everywhere. Lastly, put the carrot, courgette, corn kernels and sunflower sprouts in a bowl, and toss with the pasta sauce. Top with Grated 'Cheese' (page 52).

Like peas, corn is blanched before it is frozen, so is not raw when you buy it like this. Corn on the cob should be bought as fresh as possible, and eaten on the same day: as soon as it is picked, the sugar in the corn begins to turn to starch, and the corn loses its natural sweetness.

Serves 2
Takes 30 minutes
You need a blender, and a Spiralizer is helpful

SWEET AND SOUR

When I used to cook vegan dinners for my husband, I would sometimes buy organic ready-made sauces for convenience, and add them to a stir fry. When he started to transition to raw, I tried simply heating these same sauces and adding raw vegetables to them, but the taste was not the best! So I looked at the ingredients on the jars, and realised how simple it would be to make my own, raw sauces.

SAUCE

3 tomatoes
2 carrots
¼ red onion
60 g/2 oz dates
30 g/1 oz sun-dried tomatoes
2 tbsp apple cider vinegar
1 tsp tamari
2 tbsp extra virgin olive oil
1 cm/½ inch piece fresh ginger
1 clove garlic
¼ red chilli pepper

FILLING

3 mushrooms
1 red pepper
60 g/2 oz mange tout
2 leaves pak choi
1 slice fresh pineapple

Prepare the tomatoes, carrots and onion for the blender. Put all the sauce ingredients in together and puree for a couple of minutes to make a thick, smooth sauce. Slice the mushrooms and the pepper finely (use the slicing plate on your food processor or a mandolin if you have one). You can use the mange tout whole, or chop them into smaller pieces if you prefer. Chop the pak choi into small bite-sized pieces, and dice the pineapple. Put all the ingredients, both filling and sauce, in a bowl, and toss together. If you can, warm gently before serving, by standing in a heat-proof bowl in a pan of simmering water.

Pineapple is a valuable source of the enzyme bromelain, which is an anti-inflammatory reputed to help relief from health issues such as arthritis and colitis.

Serves 2
Takes 30 minutes
You need a blender

THAI GREEN CURRY

For red curry, substitute spinach in Thai soup recipe for 1 red pepper. For yellow curry, try a yellow pepper. Turmeric always helps turn things yellow as well.

1 portion Thai soup (page 34)
90 g/3 oz mung bean sprouts (see page 18)
4 mushrooms
90 g/3 oz green beans
150 g/5 oz broccoli
5 baby corn

Serves 2 // Takes 30 minutes
You need a blender

Slice the mushrooms, green beans, broccoli and baby corn into small bite-sized pieces. Reserve one sliced mushroom, and put the rest of the vegetables in a bowl with the sprouts and soup and mix together. Garnish with the remaining mushroom and serve.

Green beans are sprayed with over 60 pesticides – buy organic ones if you can. You can look online for lists of foods that are sprayed the most and the least, so you can make informed decisions when you are doing your shopping.

THAI YELLOW CURRY

I made this recipe for my food prep classes in 2011. I think it's one of the most well received recipes I've ever created. When I have a café, this will be on the menu for sure. It's even better if you can warm it up gently. I like to use kelp noodles, but if you can't get them, just spiralize a courgette instead.

1 packet kelp noodles
2 tomatoes
1 yellow pepper
¼ red onion
2 sticks celery
1 carrot
1 date
2 tbsp lecithin
2 tbsp coconut oil
1 tbsp apple cider vinegar
1 tsp turmeric
½ tsp chilli powder
1 tsp yellow curry paste
1 tsp tamari
4 mushrooms
100 g/3½ oz baby spinach leaves

Serves 4
Takes 15 minutes. Best if you can marinade for at least 4 hours before serving.
You need a blender

Ideally, you need to marinate kelp noodles for four hours before serving. If you've got time, the best thing to do is to make the sauce and marinade them straight into the sauce. If you haven't got time, then I recommend marinating them just in some olive oil and apple cider vinegar beforehand and then pouring the sauce on once you've made it.

To make the sauce, first prepare your tomatoes, pepper, onion, celery, carrot and date for the blender. Put them all in together and give them a quick whiz. Then add the lecithin, coconut oil, apple cider vinegar, turmeric, chilli, curry paste and tamari and blend again until smooth. Transfer to a large mixing bowl. Fine slice your mushrooms and add that into the bowl. Tip in your baby spinach leaves, and stir those in. Put your kelp noodles in as well and give it all a good stir. Warm gently before serving, either in a porringer, Thermomix, or heat-proof bowl stood in a pan of simmering water. Keeps well in the fridge for at least three days.

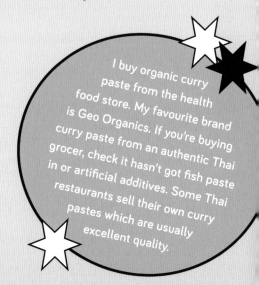

I buy organic curry paste from the health food store. My favourite brand is Geo Organics. If you're buying curry paste from an authentic Thai grocer, check it hasn't got fish paste in or artificial additives. Some Thai restaurants sell their own curry pastes which are usually excellent quality.

ALMOND, CAULIFLOWER AND CHICK PEA CURRY

What makes Asian food special is not so much the way it is cooked but the beautiful blend of ingredients they use. I used to think that I could never go completely raw because I would miss take away treats too much – now we eat Indian, Thai, or Chinese style whenever we choose.

125 g/4 oz almonds, soaked 4-8 hours
250 ml/8 fl oz water
125 g/4 oz spinach
¼ red onion
1 tsp miso
1 tsp curry paste
¼ red chilli pepper
125 g/4 oz chick pea sprouts (see page 18)
3 mushrooms, sliced
150 g/5 oz cauliflower, chopped
½ stick celery, chopped
60 g/2 oz fresh green peas
2 tbsp almonds

Pre-soak your almonds for at least four hours. In the blender, process the almonds and water to a milk. If you have a milk bag, you can strain the milk to make your dish smoother and creamier. If not, you can just strain it through a sieve. Discard the pulp. Put the milk back in the blender, and gradually add the spinach until it has become a thick green liquid. Add the onion, miso, curry paste and chilli and blend again until smooth. Next, slice the mushrooms, cauliflower and celery into small bite-sized pieces. In a bowl, mix the sauce with the sprouts, mushrooms, cauliflower, celery, peas and remaining almonds so they are evenly covered. Serve with a sliced mushroom or a sprig of coriander for garnish.

Frozen peas are blanched before freezing, so are not raw. If you have time, buy peas in the pod and shell them yourself – raw peas are much crunchier and taste quite different.

Serves 2 // Takes 30 minutes, with 4-8 hours pre-soaking for the almonds
You need a blender

TOMATO AND ASPARAGUS CURRY

Asparagus is a member of the lily family that also includes onions and garlic.
It has been cultivated for more than 2,000 years; the ancient Greeks and Romans
ate it, and also used it as a medicine. English asparagus has a very short season in April
and May; outside of this time, it may be preferable to substitute another vegetable, rather
than use imported asparagus which will not be as fresh and flavoursome.

3 tomatoes
6 sun-dried tomatoes
1 stick celery
1 carrot
1 tsp tamari
2 tbsp extra virgin olive oil
¼ red onion
1 tbsp garam masala
¼ red chilli pepper
1 carrot, sliced
6 asparagus spears, sliced
3 mushrooms, sliced
60 g/2 oz spinach, shredded
60 g/2 oz lentil sprouts (see page 18)
2 tbsp cashews

To make the sauce, put the tomatoes, sun-dried tomatoes, celery, carrot, tamari, extra virgin olive oil, onion, garam masala and chilli in the blender. Blend for a minute until you have a thick smooth sauce. With a vegetable peeler, peel the remaining carrot from top to bottom to make carrot ribbons. Keep peeling until you have used as much of the carrot as you can (finely chop the remainder). Or use a Spiralizer or mandolin if you have one. Next, slice the asparagus and mushroom into small bite-sized pieces, and shred the spinach into small strips. In a bowl, mix all your vegetables, sprouts, and cashews into the sauce so the ingredients are evenly covered. Serve garnished with lentil sprouts. Warm gently before serving if you can: the easiest way is in a heat-proof bowl stood in a pan of simmering water.

Garam masala is Indian for 'warming spices', and adds heat to a dish without being overly spicy. There are many different variations of garam masala available, usually made with a mixture of black pepper, cumin, chilli, fennel, cloves, coriander, cardamom, and nutmeg.

Serves 2 // Takes 30 minutes // You need a blender

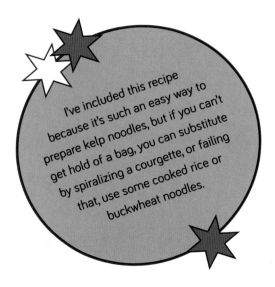

I've included this recipe because it's such an easy way to prepare kelp noodles, but if you can't get hold of a bag, you can substitute by spiralizing a courgette, or failing that, use some cooked rice or buckwheat noodles.

POTTED KELP NOODLES

Not quite as instant as a Pot Noodle, but close. Only got 10 minutes? I promise you can make a gourmet raw meal worthy of a 5 star restaurant. You will have to leave them to marinade of course – you could eat them straight away but they are much better after a few hours.

100 g/3½ oz mushrooms
1 red pepper
1 packet kelp noodles
2 tbsp tahini
125 ml/4 fl oz extra virgin olive oil
125 ml/4 fl oz water
1 tbsp tamari
1 tbsp apple cider vinegar
1 tsp garlic powder
1 tsp sumac or other warming
  spice eg paprika, cumin

Fine slice the mushroom and pepper. Put them in a large bowl. Open the kelp noodles, rinse them well, and cut them up with scissors. Put them in the bowl with the vegetables. In a separate smaller bowl, mix up the tahini, olive oil, water, tamari and apple cider vinegar with a whisk or a fork. Pour this mixture over the noodles and vegetables. Stir in the garlic powder and sumac. Mix it all together, cover, and leave for at least 2 hours.

Serves 2 (or 1 very hungry kelp noodle lover)
Takes 10 minutes, though marinating // time of 2 hours is recommended
No special equipment needed

CREAM OF COCONUT CURRY

Fresh coconut is a vital component of a raw food diet, being one of the few plant sources of saturated fats. However, coconut oil does not increase cholesterol levels like the saturated fats found in animal products, but on the contrary, is one of the most health-giving oils available, being very similar in its make-up to the fats in mother's milk. Lauric acid, the main fatty acid in coconuts (and mother's milk) has antiviral and antibacterial properties.

100 g/3½ oz creamed coconut
½ avocado
2 dates
3 tomatoes
1 carrot
¼ red onion
1 tsp tamari
1 tsp curry paste
¼ red chilli pepper
125 ml/4 fl oz water
60 g/2 oz sunflower sprouts (see page 18)
2 tbsp raisins
1 stick celery, finely chopped
1 carrot, finely chopped
¼ daikon, grated
60 g/2 oz cauliflower, finely chopped

Blend the coconut, avocado, dates, tomatoes, carrot, onion, tamari, curry paste, chilli pepper and water, to make a smooth sauce. Dice the celery, carrot, daikon and cauliflower, and transfer them to a large bowl. Mix in the sauce so the vegetables are evenly coated. Garnish with carrot ribbons (see page 94).

When buying brown coconuts, shake it to hear the liquid inside: the more it has sloshing around, the fresher it is.

Serves 2
Takes 30 minutes
You need a blender

Puddings

BANANA SPLIT

In my early days of raw, this was one of my favourite lunches. It takes two minutes
to prepare, makes the humble banana more interesting, and really hits the spot.

2 bananas
1 tbsp nut butter – hemp or tahini
   are good (see page 38)
handful raisins or goji berries
handful sunflower or pumpkin
   seeds

Serves 1 // Takes 5 minutes //
You don't need any equipment

Peel the bananas and slice in half lengthways. Spread each inside edge with nut butter and then cover with dried fruit and seeds. Sandwich the two halves together, and serve.

Darwin proposed that bananas were man's perfect food. They come in a disposable, biodegradable wrapping, that changes colour to indicate ripeness. They are shaped to fit snugly in our hands, and contain every nutrient the body needs.

APPLE SANDWICH
A fruitarian sandwich!

1 apple
1 tbsp nut butter
Topping of choice e.g. sliced grapes,
   dates, berries, raisins, goji berries

Serves 1 // Takes 5 minutes
You don't need any special
equipment

Slice the apple into 0.5 cm/¼ inch slices crossways through the core, so you get circular pieces with beautiful star patterns in the centre. Spread each slice on one side with the nut butter of your choice. Top with thinly sliced fruits, and eat as it is, or sandwich another piece of apple on top.

I like to use Lexia raisins rather than standard Muscatel raisins. Lexias are made from a different variety of grape, and are plumper and juicier.

DATES AND TAHINI

This may sound simple, but it can't be beaten for taste. In my early raw days, settling down
with a jar of tahini and a box of fresh dates was one of my favourite comfort foods: very
sweet and rich, a good chocolate substitute, and there's no preparation necessary. Currently, I
recommend Sun and Seed as the best quality raw nut butters in the UK, and I like the Iranian
dates that come packed in cardboard boxes in a lot of grocers and whole food stores.

Fresh dates
Raw tahini

Serves 1 // No preparation or
equipment necessary

Remove the stones from the dates and replace with half a teaspoon of tahini.

Date stones can be grown into houseplants – just plant the stone vertically in compost, and keep it in a warm place until shoots appear.

BEST FRUIT SALAD

Another recipe that shouldn't be overlooked because of its simplicity.
I used to love having a fruit meal for lunch, and there are so many permutations
of fruit salad, you will never tire of it. Also makes a fun breakfast.

3 pieces fresh fruit
½ apple, grated
1 banana, thinly sliced
1 tbsp raisins
dressing

Chop your favourite fruits into tiny pieces and in a bowl, mix together with the apple, banana and raisins. For a plain salad, sprinkle with lemon juice and grated coconut; for a richer dessert, cover with carob sauce (page 22) or cashew cream (page 143). Or you can try banana ice cream (page 110), or live yoghurt.

Some good combinations are:
guava, kiwi, and strawberry; mango, papaya and strawberry; pineapple and mango. In the autumn, try buying different varieties of apples, and mixing them together.

Serves 1-2
Takes 10 minutes
You don't need any special
equipment

Research repeatedly shows that a diet high in nutrients and low in calories reduces the risk of serious disease and slows the ageing process.

COMFORT APPLE SAUCE

More comfort food! This makes a great breakfast. Or sprinkle with granola for instant apple crumble.

500 g/1 lb apple, chopped
60 g/2 oz raisins, pre-soaked
125 g/4 oz fresh dates or prunes
1 tsp cinnamon

Pre-soak the raisins for an hour to soften them (drink the soak water, it's delicious). Core and dice the apple, and put everything in the blender. Blend to a puree.

Raw food preparation relies heavily on the use of a high power blender, and a dehydrator. If you are serious about eating raw, they are well worth investing in. However, they are expensive pieces of equipment, and before I had either of them I used to read raw food recipe books and get very frustrated by the amount of recipes that I was precluded from. Consequently, wherever possible I have tried to offer alternative methods when these pieces of equipment are used.

Serves 4
Takes 10 minutes, with 1 hour
pre-soaking
You need a blender

PEAR AND CINNAMON YOGHURT

You can serve this as it is, or alternatively blend for a pureed pudding.
You can substitute any fruit for the pears – guavas work particularly well.

2 pears, chopped
2 tbsp raisins or goji
  berries
2 tbsp live yoghurt (soya
  or goats')
1 tsp cinnamon
juice ½ lemon

Core and dice the pears. Put all the ingredients in a bowl and toss together.

Pears are among the least allergenic foods. Years ago, I flat shared with a guy who had such severe allergies, there were only about ten foods he could eat, and pears were one of them.

Serves 2 // Takes 5 minutes // You don't need any special equipment

THE FAVOURITE PUDDING

Generally, people don't think of putting avocados in sweet dishes, but the results are sublime. Avocados are actually neutral, neither sweet nor savoury, and when added to fruit make a positively ambrosial pudding. Avocado pudding in some form or other is every raw fooders' favourite dessert.

1 avocado
1 banana
1-2 pieces fresh fruit

Prepare all the ingredients for the blender. Put everything in the food processor and process to a smooth creamy puree.

VARIATIONS:
MANGO: one large mango, ½ lemon
COCONUT: one apple, 1 tbsp raisins, 1 tbsp grated coconut
PEACH AND REDCURRANT: one large peach, 2 tbsp redcurrants
BLACKBERRY AND APPLE: one apple, 2 tbsp blackberries
CHOCOLATE (my favourite – a truly ambrosial pudding): 125 g/4 oz fresh dates (if using dried soak for a few hours to soften), 1 tbsp cacao powder

Serves 2 // Takes 10 minutes // You need a blender

The name avocado comes from the Aztec ahuacatl (meaning testicle), probably due of the fruit's shape, and because it was thought to be an aphrodisiac.

TROPICAL FRUIT PUDDING

There are an incredible number of tropical fruits that we rarely see in this country. Unfortunately, by the time they reach the UK, many are past their best; naturally, fruit tastes best when ripe and freshly picked. This pudding contains tropical fruits that are more widely available; they may have been exotic to our grandparents but now they are positively commonplace. It makes a rich, luxurious dessert, appropriate for special occasions.

2 avocados
1 banana
1 guava
1 mango
½ papaya
1 tbsp dried coconut flakes

Serves 2 // Takes 10 minutes
You need a blender

Prepare all the ingredients for your blender by chopping them into small enough pieces. Scoop the flesh out of the avocados, peel the banana, slice the mango off the stone and remove the peel. Slice the papaya in half, remove the seeds, and scoop out the flesh. I usually use all of the guava, skin, seeds and all. Put them in the blender and process to a smooth creamy puree. Top with grated coconut.

Papaya contains the enzyme papain, which aids digestion. There are over 500 varieties of mango, which is also known as the apple of the tropics, and a quality source of vitamins A and C.

MANGO SORBET

Luscious sorbet, free from any sugar or artificial additives

1 mango

Serves 1
Takes 5 minutes with 24 hours
pre-freezing
You need a food processor

Peel and slice mango, place in a plastic bag and freeze for 24 hours. When you're ready to serve it, break it down in the food processor or high power blender to make a smooth puree.

Many fruits sold in supermarkets are picked unripe, to make it easier to transport and store them. Fruit that has not been given a chance to fully ripen is not as flavourful as fruit that has naturally matured, and will be lacking in vital phytonutrients.

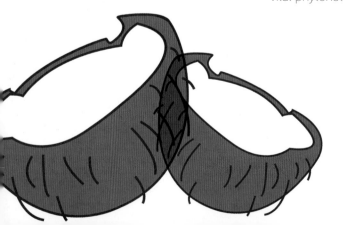
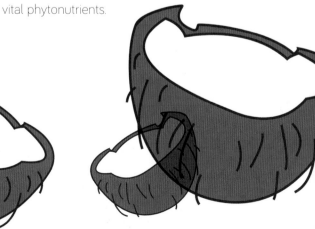

STRAWBERRY MOUSSE

It's no secret that I'm a big fan of Irish moss. I love my desserts, and I love my sea vegetables, so a dish that combines both is my idea of heaven. Of course, if strawberries aren't in season you can substitute for any other fruit you can find; in the winter months I often buy frozen organic berries for these kind of recipes. If you're interested in experimenting more, there's a lot of Irish moss recipes on my Kate's Magic Bubble site.

100 g/3½ oz cashews,
   pre-soaked
30 g/1 oz Irish moss
750 ml/24 fl oz water
1 tbsp raw honey
2 tbsp lecithin granules
2 tbsp coconut oil
250 g/8 oz strawberries

Irish moss is popular as a thickener in desserts. It makes light fluffy cakes and puddings, which everyone loves. It's a great source of bone-building minerals, and as long as you prepare your Irish moss properly, your dessert won't taste of seaweed at all.

Serves 4
Takes 15 minutes, but you need to pre-soak your cashews 4-8 hours and pre-soak your Irish moss for at least 3 days
You need a blender

Pre-soak the cashews for 4-8 hours. Soak the Irish moss according to manufacturer's instructions. I use the Spanish brand, Algamar. You need to rinse it well to remove any shells or lichen. Then put it in water in an airtight container in the fridge and leave for at least three days. If you don't leave it long enough, it won't gel your recipe. If you leave it too long, it will start going smelly! If you don't use it within a week, then you will need to chuck it away.

When you're ready to use it, remove from the soak water. It's important you discard the soak water, as this has a fishy taste. It's equally important you don't rinse the seaweed because then you will wash away the gelling agent.

In your blender or food processor, blend the Irish moss with one cup (250 ml/8 fl oz) of the water. Blend it as much as you can, so the seaweed bits are as broken down as much as you can get them. You don't have to worry too much because it will blend down more in the next stage. Next add the honey, lecithin, coconut oil, cashews, and strawberries. Blend to a puree; it should be very thick at this point. Gradually add the remaining 500 ml of water.

Pour into a large mould or serving dish, and put it in the fridge to set; it will take at least 6 hours to thicken nicely. Keeps in the fridge in an airtight container for up to five days.

BANANA ICE CREAM

This is one of the most popular raw desserts. It's so simple to make and an exquisite fat-free alternative to dairy ice cream. We used to have it as a breakfast treat as well: bananas are very filling and sustaining and a great source of nutrients. In fact there is even a group of raw foodists who subscribe to the belief of eating 30 bananas a day! Not something I would advocate personally, especially in our cold UK climate.

2 bananas per person. The average food processor can hold up to 8 bananas

Peel the bananas, break into chunks and place in a plastic bag. Freeze for 24 hours – I have a permanent supply on hand in the freezer. It's a good recipe for those nearly black ones that you need to use up before they become too over-ripe to eat. When the boys were little they would often only eat half a banana and the other half would go in the freezer. When you are ready to serve the ice cream, remove the chunks from the freezer and put them in the food processor. It takes a good few minutes for them to break down – when the ice cream is smooth and creamy it is ready.

VARIATIONS:

Add when blending (per single serving):

VANILLA: 1 tbsp tahini, 1 tsp vanilla powder

CAROB: 1 tbsp carob powder, 1 tbsp almond butter

MINT chop chip: 3 drops peppermint oil and 20g (^{2}/$_3$ oz) raw chocolate, grated

FRUIT AND NUT: 1 tbsp chopped, dried fruit, 1 tbsp chopped nuts

BERRY: just a handful of berries adds a strong flavour e.g. strawberry, blackberry, blueberry

PEACH: one peach and 1 tbsp tahini

CHOCOLATE: 1 tbsp cacao powder, 1 tbsp agave

Booja Booja do an excellent raw ice cream that you can find in health food stores. Also if you like your chocolate, you need to check out their raw chocolate truffles.

Serves 1
Takes 5 minutes with 24 hours pre-freezing time
You need a food processor

Cakes and Tarts

FRIDGE CAKE

This recipe makes a lot, but it keeps well, and never seems to last long in our house.
You may want to halve it, if it's just for you. For chocolate fridge cake,
substitute cacao powder for the carob.

125 g/4 oz rolled oats, soaked 4-8
  hours
250 g/8 oz almonds, ground
60 g/2 oz coconut flakes, ground
250 g/8 oz dates (dried rather
  than fresh)
250 g/8 oz raisins
250 g/8 oz sultanas
30 g/1 oz carob powder
1 tbsp grain coffee
4 tbsp yacon syrup
2 tsp mixed spice

ICING
250 g/8 oz tahini
5-6 tbsp agave
30 g/1 oz carob powder
125 ml/4 fl oz water

Makes 25 squares
Takes 40 minutes with 12 hours
pre-soaking
You need a food processor

Pre-soak the oats for 4-8 hours. Grind the almonds and coconut flakes. Break down the dates, raisins and sultanas in the food processor, until they form a homogenized mass. Set aside. Next, put the oats in the food processor, and process until they are mashed completely, with no individual grains discernible. Add the dried fruit back into the food processor along with the almonds and coconut, and process until the oats, dried fruit and nuts are evenly mixed, resulting in a thick, sticky mass. Transfer this to a mixing bowl, and add the rest of the ingredients by hand, stirring with a wooden spoon until thoroughly mixed. Then press it into a 24 cm (9½ inch) square tray.

To make the icing, put the tahini and agave in a bowl and stir with a spoon. Add the carob powder and then add the water gradually. For some reason when you add water to tahini it makes it thicker! So just add the water a little at a time, and it won't make your icing too runny. When it is completely mixed in, spread the icing over the top of the fridge cake. Leave it in a fridge for a few hours to harden, then slice it into squares (five up by five down).

I believe the version of this you find in health food stores and cafés is raw apart from the use of rolled oats.

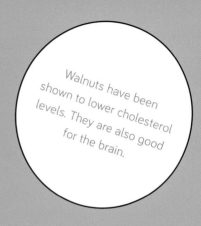

Walnuts have been shown to lower cholesterol levels. They are also good for the brain.

CRUMBLE CAKE

If you don't have a dehydrator, leave this cake in the oven at the lowest temperature possible for a few hours to warm through.

CRUMBLE
125 g/4 oz almonds, pre-soaked
150 g/5 oz walnuts, pre-soaked
125 g/4 oz rolled oats, pre-soaked
5-6 tbsp agave

FRUIT
125 g/4 oz dates or dried apricots
125 g/4 oz apple
1 tsp cinnamon

Pre-soak the almonds, walnuts and oats for 4-8 hours. Make the crumble and fruit mixtures as detailed in the apple crumble recipe (next page). Divide the crumble into two equal halves, and press one half onto a dehydrator sheet. Spread the fruit mixture over the first layer of crumble, and press a second layer of crumble over the top. Dehydrate for about four hours. When it's done, cut it into squares (four up by four down). Stored in the fridge, it will keep for up to a week.

Makes 16 squares
Takes 30 minutes, with 4-8 hours pre-soaking, and 4 hours dehydrating
You need a food processor, and a blender,
and a dehydrator is helpful although you can use an oven

APPLE CRUMBLE

Apple crumble is about as traditionally English as it gets; it was always one of my favourite desserts, and I was determined that just because I was on a raw diet I wasn't going to miss out on it.

CRUMBLE
125 g/4 oz almonds, pre-soaked
150 g/5 oz walnuts, pre-soaked
125 g/4 oz rolled oats, pre-soaked
5-6 tbsp agave syrup

FILLING
125 g/4 oz raisins
1 kg/2 lb apples
1 tbsp cinnamon

Pre-soak the almonds, walnuts and oats for 4-8 hours. To make the crumble, break down the almonds and walnuts in the food processor until they are in evenly sized pieces, about the size of rice grains. Add the rolled oats, and process until they are about the same size. Lastly, add the agave and process briefly, so that you have a thick, lumpy mass, the same sort of consistency as traditional crumble. Set aside.

Blend all the filling ingredients together in a blender until you have a puree. Line a 23 cm (9 inch) serving dish with the apple and cover with crumble. If you have a dehydrator you can warm it in there for a few hours before serving. Serve with Cashew Cream (page 143) or Banana Ice Cream (page 110).

All oats bought in the shops are heat-treated to stabilise them. To the best of my knowledge, Raw Living sells the only truly raw oats available in the UK, and even our supply is very sporadic, so they can be out of stock for long periods of time.

Serves 8
Takes 40 minutes, with 4-8 hours pre-soaking
You need a food processor and a blender

RAW CHEESECAKE

This is a basic cake crust that can be used in any raw dish as a replacement for the standard pastry case. It makes a moderately thick crust, which will line the sides and base of the tin. Personally, I prefer a thinner crust which just lines the base, and so often use just 125 g/4 oz each of almonds and dates. If on the other hand, you like a really thick crust, use 250 g/8 oz of each.

Baobab is one of my favourite ingredients. It is a South African superfruit which is full of anti-oxidants, vitamins and minerals. But I love it the most for its subtle lemony flavour, and it also helps thicken recipes. If you don't have it, you could just substitute the juice of one lemon.

BASE
180 g/6 oz almonds, soaked 4-8 hours
180 g/6 oz dried dates
2 tsp cinnamon

FILLING
250 g/8 oz cashews, soaked 4-8 hours
125 g/4 oz coconut oil
4 tbsp agave syrup
1 tbsp vanilla powder
250 ml/8 fl oz water
1 tbsp Baobab (optional)

TOPPING:
100-200 g/3-7 oz fresh fruits e.g. berries, peach slices

Serves 8
Takes 45 minutes with 4-8 hours pre-soaking, and minimum 2 hours setting time
You need a blender and food processor

Pre-soak the almonds and cashews for 4-8 hours. In the food processor, grind the almonds as fully as possible. Add the dates and cinnamon and mix until they have formed one solid mass. You may need to add a drop or two of water to make it stick; no more or it will go soggy. Use this mixture to line the base and sides of a 23 cm (9 inch) cake tin. If you're using a traditional cake tin, I suggest lining it with greaseproof paper, silver foil or cling film so it turns out easily. You may want to invest in silicon moulds as they are perfect for raw cakes and you don't need to line them.

Put the soaked cashews, coconut oil, agave and vanilla powder in the blender, adding the water gradually. Leave to set in the fridge for at least a few hours. Top with whatever fresh fruit is in season. Alternatively, top with Chocolate Spread (page 144).

You can also vary this by adding ingredients to the actual cheesecake mixture e.g. chocolate cheesecake, strawberry cheesecake. At Raw Living, we sell a range of fruit powders, such as blueberry and raspberry, which are perfect for this. Or you can use essential oils, for example orange oil for an orange cheesecake.

CARROT CAKE

If you can get it, use organic cinnamon, the flavour is far superior. It took me a long while to realise that it was worth paying the extra for all organic ingredients, not just the basics. When I started to buy organic herbs and spices it was a revelation – the tastes are more delicate and subtle, and bring out the flavours in a dish rather than overpower them.

300 g/10 oz walnuts, pre-soaked
6 large carrots
100 g/3½ oz coconut flakes
1 cm/½ inch piece fresh ginger
125 g/4 oz fresh dates
60 g/2 oz raisins
60 g/2 oz dried apricots
1 tbsp cinnamon
½ tsp nutmeg powder

ICING
125 g/4 oz cashews, soaked for
   4-8 hours
200 g/6½ oz raisins, soaked for
   1-2 hours
1 tbsp vanilla powder
125 ml/4 fl oz water

Pre-soak walnuts for 4-8 hours. Juice the carrots. Drink the juice and remove the pulp from the juicer. In the food processor, process the walnuts, coconut, ginger, dates, apricots and raisins. You may have to do this in stages, depending how powerful your machine is. Once they are as broken down as you can get them, transfer the mix to a large bowl, and, using a wooden spoon, stir in the carrot pulp and the spices until they are thoroughly and evenly blended. Press into a 23 cm (9 inch) cake tin. If you're using a traditional cake tin, I suggest lining it with greaseproof paper, silver foil or cling film so it turns out easily. You may want to invest in silicon moulds as they are perfect for raw cakes and you don't need to line them.

To make the icing, make sure you've pre-soaked the cashews and raisins. Put all the ingredients in the blender, adding as little water as possible to make the icing thick (start with 4 tbsp, and add the rest gradually). Spread the icing over the carrot cake, and leave in the fridge for at least a few hours. The cake will keep for about a week – the flavours improve with age.

In Roman times, carrots were yellow and purple. The modern orange carrot was developed by Dutch farmers, who thought it would be funny to develop a carrot the colour of their national flag. However rainbow carrots are now making something of a comeback and are available in some selected supermarkets and farmers' markets.

Serves 8
Pre-soaking 4-8 hours, takes 45 minutes,
minimum 2 hours setting time
You need a food processor and a blender

ICE-CREAM CAKE

For variations, see Banana Ice Cream (page 110). This is a lovely one to make in the summer, as it keeps indefinitely. I break chunks off, and snack on it straight from the freezer. Or keep it on hand to serve surprise guests.

CRUST

125 g/4 oz almonds, soaked
   4-8 hours
125 g/4 oz dried dates
2 tsp cinnamon

TOPPING

8 bananas, broken into
   pieces and frozen at least
   24 hours beforehand
1 tbsp agave syrup
2 tbsp tahini
1 tbsp raisins

Serves 12
Takes 45 minutes, with 4-8
hours pre-soaking and 24
hours pre-freezing
You need a food processor or
high power blender

In the food processor, grind the almonds as fully as possible. Add the dates and cinnamon and mix until they have formed one solid mass. You may need to add a drop or two of water to make it stick; no more or it will go soggy. Use this mixture to line the base and sides of a 23 cm (9 inch) cake tin. If you're using a traditional cake tin, I suggest lining it with greaseproof paper, silver foil or cling film so it turns out easily. You may want to invest in silicon moulds as they are perfect for raw cakes and you don't need to line them.

Put the bananas in the food processor (it will take a few minutes for them to break down this way – when the ice cream is smooth and creamy it is ready). Add the agave, tahini, and raisins to the bananas and mix them in with a wooden spoon. Spoon the ice cream onto the base and serve immediately. Store the leftovers in the freezer. You can eat it straight from the freezer, or defrost in the fridge for ten to fifteen minutes first, for a softer cake.

China is now the world's biggest fruit producer, followed by Brazil and the USA. For more facts like this, I recommend the website the World's Healthiest Foods. It's my go to resource for helpful info on fruits and vegetables.

FAVOURITE FRUIT TART

As the name suggests I like this very much and it is a raw food classic.
Very simple to make, and with so many variations, you will never tire of it.
A welcome introduction to raw foods to impress cynical guests.

CRUST
180 g/6 oz almonds, soaked 8-12
   hours
180 g/6 oz dried dates
2 tsp ground cinnamon

FILLING
4-6 pieces fresh fruit (see method)
1 large banana
2 tbsp dates
2 tbsp tahini
juice 1 lemon

Serves 12
Takes 45 minutes to make, with 4-8
hours pre-soaking
You need a food processor and a
blender

In the food processor, grind the almonds as fully as possible. Add the dates and cinnamon and mix until they have formed one solid mass. You may need to add a drop or two of water to make it stick; no more or it will go soggy. Use this mixture to line the base and sides of a 23 cm (9 inch) cake tin. If you're using a traditional cake tin, I suggest lining it with greaseproof paper, silver foil or cling film so it turns out easily. You may want to invest in silicon moulds as they are perfect for raw cakes and you don't need to line them.

Blend the banana, dates, tahini and lemon juice in the blender, until they form a thick sauce with no lumps left. Pour the sauce over the base, spreading it evenly into all the nooks and crannies.

Slice your fresh fruit and arrange decoratively over the sauce. Try mango, kiwi, papaya, peach, strawberry, plain old apple, or any mixture that you fancy – like mixed berries for a summer tart, or mango, papaya and guava for a tropical tart.

Serve immediately – and try not to eat it all at once! For a richer, creamier tart, you may like to double the amount of sauce, so that the fruit is smothered in it rather than just lightly coated.

The top five overall most nutritious fruits are guava, watermelon, grapefruit, kiwi, and papaya.

SECRET 'CHOCOLATE' TORTE

This has to be tasted to be believed; it makes an amazing deep chocolatey dessert. Serve this to your guests and see if anyone can guess the secret ingredient – they will not believe you when you tell them.

CRUST
200 g/ 6½ oz coconut flakes
125 g/4 oz almonds
1 tbsp raw honey
4 tbsp water

FILLING
300 g/10 oz plain black olives, pitted
450 g/14½ oz fresh dates
30 g/1 oz carob powder
1 tbsp grain coffee
1 tbsp ground cinnamon
1 tbsp vanilla powder
180 ml/6 fl oz water
2 tbsp powdered psyllium husks

Serves 12
Takes 30 minutes
You need a food processor

To make the crust, chop the coconut in the food processor until it is completely broken down. Add the almonds and process until they are mixed together. Spoon in the honey, and pour the water in a little at a time, just enough to hold it all together. Use to line the base of a 23 cm (9 inch) cake tin. If you're using a traditional cake tin, I suggest lining it with greaseproof paper, silver foil or cling film so it turns out easily. You may want to invest in silicon moulds as they are perfect for raw cakes and you don't need to line them.

To make the filling, break down the olives in the food processor. Add the dates and process until a paste is formed. Then add the carob, grain coffee, cinnamon and vanilla, and blend thoroughly. Keep the machine running, and pour in the water. Finally, add the psyllium gradually, while the machine is on. After a minute, turn the machine off, and immediately spoon the mixture onto the coconut base before the psyllium starts to set. Spread out evenly with a knife, and leave in the fridge for a few hours to firm.

Like avocados, black olives have a surprisingly neutral flavour, and work well with fruit. It's vital that you use plain, black pitted olives that have been soaked in brine rather than marinated in any oils and herbs etc. that will contaminate the flavour.

MINCEMEAT TART

If you are trying to eat raw at Christmas time, it is very hard not to be tempted
unless you have your own treats to succumb to instead.
The following three recipes will amply satisfy lovers of traditional fare.

CRUST
180 g/6 oz almonds, soaked
  4-8 hours
180 g/6 oz dried dates
2 tsp cinnamon

MINCEMEAT
1 orange
1 lemon
350 g/12 oz grated apple
125 g/4 oz Lexia raisins
125 g/4 oz sultanas
125 g/4 oz currants
60 g/2 oz dates, chopped
1 tbsp ground cinnamon
1 tsp ground ginger
pinch ground nutmeg
pinch ground cloves
2 tbsp flaxseed oil
1 tbsp agave syrup
1 tbsp yacon syrup
1 tsp miso

Pre-soak the almonds for 4-8 hours. In the food processor, grind the almonds as fully as possible. Add the dates and cinnamon and mix until they have formed one solid mass. You may need to add a drop or two of water to make it stick; no more or it will go soggy. Use this mixture to line the base and sides of a 23 cm (9 inch) cake tin.

Juice the lemon and the orange, and grate the rind. Grate the apple. Mix all the mincemeat ingredients together in a large bowl. Use a wooden spoon, and make sure everything is evenly mixed. Press the mincemeat into the crust. If you can bear not to tuck in straight away, leave it in the fridge for at least a few hours to allow the flavours to mingle, and serve with Cashew Cream (page 143) or Banana Ice Cream (page 110). It keeps well in the fridge, for a week or two (if given the chance).

Use organic, unwaxed lemons and oranges. Non-organic fruits are covered in an inedible wax that makes them more shiny and so supposedly more desirable to the consumer.

Serves 8
Takes 30 minutes, with 4-8 hours pre-soaking
You need a food processor

CHRISTMAS CAKE

This takes some time to prepare, and is very rich,
but will allow you to feel suitably decadent when you tuck in on Christmas day.

CAKE
150 g/5 oz walnuts
125 g/4 oz almonds
250 g/8 oz dried figs
60 g/2 oz dates
60 g/2 oz dried apricots
60 g/2 oz raisins
60 g/2 oz currants
1 tbsp yacon syrup
1 orange, juiced
1 tsp miso
1 tbsp cinnamon powder
1 tsp ginger powder
pinch grated nutmeg
pinch ground cloves

MARZIPAN
200 g/ 6½ oz almond butter
3 tbsp agave syrup
1 tbsp vanilla powder

ICING
200 g/ 6½ oz coconut oil
125 g/4 oz dates

Serves 12
Takes 1 hour to make
You need a grinder and food
processor

You need a powerful food processor for this one. First, you need to grind the nuts and transfer them to a mixing bowl. Break down the figs until they form a homogenized mass, and transfer them to the bowl. Then break down the dates, apricots, raisins, and currants until they form a thick paste with no individual ingredients discernible, and transfer them to the bowl as well.

Add the remaining ingredients and mix thoroughly with a wooden spoon until the ingredients are completely amalgamated. Line a deep 19 cm (7½ inch) cake tin with greaseproof paper and fill it with the cake mixture (or use a silicon mould if you have one big enough). Leave it in the fridge for a few hours to harden.

To make the marzipan, add the vanilla to the almond butter and mix in. Add the agave gradually until a thick paste is formed. Turn the cake out from the tin or mould, and spread a thin layer of the marzipan over the top and sides of the cake. It is better to have some marzipan left over than to make it too thick.

To make the icing, process the dates in a food processor. Fresh dates are best but be sure to remove all the stones carefully first. Put the coconut oil in the food processor with the dates and process again until it is blended. Ice the cake while the coconut is still soft, using just enough to cover the marzipan layer – again, don't use it all unless you have to (the remainder can be rolled into balls and eaten as sweets).

Leave overnight to set. This cake will keep for a good few weeks, if given a chance.

This is adapted from a recipe that was in the first *Get Fresh* magazine I ever received, in 1993. I made it for many years, and I would always think that it was such a big cake I would never eat it all. Of course, there was never any left by January.

CHRISTMAS PUDDING

Both Christmas cake and Christmas pudding contain mostly dried fruit and spices, so it is easy to replicate raw versions.

250 g/8 oz dried figs
125 g/4 oz almonds
60 g/2 oz dates
60 g/2 oz dried apricots
60 g/2 oz raisins
60 g/2 oz currants
1 tbsp yacon syrup
2 tbsp agave syrup
1 orange, juiced
1 tsp miso
1 tbsp ground cinnamon
1 tsp ground ginger
pinch ground nutmeg
pinch ground cloves

Makes 8 small puddings
Takes 30 minutes to make, with 4 hours dehydrating
You need a grinder and a food processor. A dehydrator is helpful but not necessary.

Grind the almonds and transfer them to a mixing bowl. Break down the figs in a food processor or high power blender until they form a homogenized mass, and transfer them to the bowl. Then break down the dates, apricots, raisins, and currants together, until they form a thick paste with no individual ingredients discernible, and transfer them to the bowl as well. Next, add in the remaining ingredients and mix thoroughly with a wooden spoon until all the ingredients are completely amalgamated. On a dehydrator tray, shape into eight small Christmas puddings, and dehydrate for four hours. Serve warm, straight from the dehydrator (if you don't have a dehydrator, you can eat them just as they are).

We don't pre-soak the nuts in these recipes because we want them to have a good rich, dense texture and flavour. Most people aren't so sensitive that they can't handle small amounts of unsoaked nuts like this. However, don't eat too much in one go or you may find yourself with indigestion. If you do have a very sensitive digestion and you want to enjoy these recipes, you can soak your nuts and dehydrate them prior to grinding them. This activates them and makes them easier on the body, although obviously it's time consuming as well, so not something I personally bother with.

Breads, Biscuits and Cookies

ESSENE BREAD

The seeds and wheat grain in this loaf together form a complete protein. This is not the sort of bread you can easily slice and spread or make a sandwich with. Much better to just break chunks off, dab on a little tahini, and just eat it as it is.

150 g/5 oz wheat, sprouted (see page 18)
125 g/4 oz dates
125 g/4 oz raisins
2 tbsp sesame seeds, soaked
2 tbsp sunflower seeds, soaked
2 tbsp pumpkin seeds, soaked
2 tsp cinnamon

Makes 1 small loaf // Takes 15 minutes, with 18 hours drying time. You also need to sprout the wheat and soak the seeds in advance
You need a food processor and ideally a dehydrator, although an oven will do

Make sure you've sprouted your wheat. Soak the sesame, sunflower and pumpkin seeds for at least two hours. Put all the ingredients in the food processor or high power blender. Break down as much as possible, so there are no individual ingredients discernible, just one thick mass. Shape it into a loaf about 5 cm (2 inches) high. Dehydrate for approximately 12 hours. Flip, and dehydrate for another 6 hours on the other side. If you don't have a dehydrator you can bake it in the oven at the lowest temperature. Cooking times will depend on your oven. It won't be raw this way, but it will still be healthier than conventional bread.

People that are intolerant to cooked wheat products will not encounter the same problems with sprouted wheat. This is because when the grain is sprouted, the enzymes break down the heavy, complex starches into simple sugars, proteins into amino acids, and fats into fatty acids. Therefore, they are said to be predigested.

FLAX BREAD

Flax bread is much easier than Essene bread because there's no sprouting involved, and I think it's also much tastier. You can vary it and make sweet versions or savoury – I particularly like it with olives and sun-dried tomatoes so it's reminiscent of focaccia. Here's a simple version for you to begin with, that goes equally well with a chocolate spread or some tahini dressing and alfalfa sprouts.

250 g/8 oz flaxseeds
1 tsp miso
1 tsp raw honey
2 tbsp extra virgin olive oil
250 ml/8 fl oz water

Makes 1 small loaf // Takes 15 minutes with 18 hours drying time
You need a grinder or high power blender, and ideally a dehydrator, although an oven will do

Grind your flaxseeds in a grinder or high power blender. Transfer them to a mixing bowl and stir in all the other ingredients until you have a dough, the same consistency as bread dough. Shape into a loaf about 5 cm (2 inches) high on your dehydrator tray. Make it whatever shape you like – traditional loaf shaped, circular or even heart shaped! Dry for 12 hours, then flip over and dry for a further 6 hours on the other side. Store in the fridge and eat within a week.

Golden flaxseed and brown flaxseed are no different nutritionally. The gold is sweeter and the brown is nuttier in flavour; I usually use gold. Linseed and flaxseed are the same thing.

CARROT AND RAISIN BREAD

A lovely sweet loaf. Serve with Chocolate Spread (page 144).

90 g/3 oz sprouted wheat (see
    page 18)
1½ carrots
125 g/4 oz raisins
1 tsp cinnamon
pinch ground cloves
pinch grated nutmeg

Mix the wheat sprouts, carrots, and raisins in a food processor or high power blender. Mix in the spices. Shape it into a loaf about 5 cm (2 inches) high. Dehydrate for 12 hours. Flip and dry for another 6 hours on the other side. If you don't have a dehydrator you can bake it in the oven at the lowest temperature. Cooking times will depend on your oven. It won't be raw this way, but it will still be healthy and taste great.

The Essene bread sold in the health food stores is not raw, but as it is made from sprouted wheat, it is still a healthier choice than conventional bread.

Makes 1 small loaf
Takes 15 minutes, with 18 hours dehydrating time. You also need to sprout your wheat in advance
You need a high power blender or food processor, and ideally a dehydrator, although an oven will do

HONEY BISCUITS

This is a gorgeous, golden brown biscuit – a batch never lasts more than a few days in our house.

300 g/10 oz buckwheat, sprouted
    (see page 18)
125 ml/4 fl oz extra virgin olive oil
2 tbsp agave syrup
2 tbsp raw honey or yacon syrup
2 tsp cinnamon
4 tbsp water
90 g/3 oz raisins or goji berries

Put the buckwheat in the food processor or high power blender, and process for a couple of minutes until it becomes a thick mash. Add the extra virgin olive oil, agave, yacon or honey, cinnamon and water, and blend until you have a thick batter. Next, stir in the raisins or goji berries with a spoon. Make into thin biscuit shapes around 8-10 cm (3-4 inches) in diameter, and dehydrate for about 12 hours. Flip and dry for another 6 hours on the other side.

When buying extra virgin olive oil, look for oils that are labelled as being from the first pressing only: these are the ones that should be raw. Standard cold pressed oils will have been heated in the press and so are no longer raw.

Makes about 25 biscuits
Takes 15 minutes. You need to sprout your buckwheat in advance. Takes about 18 hours to dehydrate
You need a food processor and a dehydrator

GINGER SNAPS

This is a crunchy, stimulating biscuit. Add more ginger if you are a real fan.

300 g/10 oz buckwheat, sprouted
   (see page 18)
125 ml/4 fl oz extra virgin olive oil
60 g/2 oz flaxseed, ground
125 ml/4 fl oz agave syrup
90 g/3 oz freshly grated ginger

Makes about 30 biscuits // Takes
15 minutes. You need to sprout the
buckwheat in advance. You also need
to allow 18 hours drying time //
You need a food processor or high
power blender and a dehydrator

Put the buckwheat in the food processor or high power blender, and process for a couple of minutes until you have a thick mash. Then add the remaining ingredients and blend to make a thick batter. On dehydrator trays, make into thin biscuit shapes around 8-10 cm (3-4 inches) in diameter, and dehydrate for about 12 hours. Flip and dry for another 6 hours on the other side.

Ginger is very good for the digestion, and a traditional remedy for colds. Dried ginger has a very different taste to fresh ginger, and I do not recommend using it as a substitute.

LEMON BISCUITS

A refreshing biscuit. The sweetness of the raisins counteracts the tartness of the lemon.

300 g/10 oz buckwheat, sprouted
   (see page 18)
125 ml/4 fl oz extra virgin olive oil
125 ml/4 fl oz agave syrup
1 lemon (unwaxed)
60 g/2 oz raisins

Makes about 30 biscuits // Takes
15 minutes. You need to sprout the
buckwheat in advance. Dehydrating
time is 18 hours // You need a food
processor or high power blender, and
a dehydrator

Put the buckwheat in the food processor or high power blender, and process for a couple of minutes until it becomes a mash. Add the flesh of the lemon, carefully removing any pips. Grate some lemon rind, and add one tablespoon of it into your mixture. Next add the extra virgin olive oil and agave and process to a thick batter. Stir the raisins into the batter with a spoon. On dehydrator trays, make into thin biscuit shapes around 8-10 cm (3-4 inches) in diameter, and dehydrate for about 12 hours. Flip and then dry on the other side for another 6 hours.

Extra virgin olive oil is the only oil that is suitable for human consumption in its natural state; all other oils need to go through some kind of treatment to make them edible. Olives are a fruit, so extra virgin olive oil is really just fruit juice!

FIGGY BISCUITS

These biscuits are perfect for taking out with you on a day trip or to work, as they are not so crumbly as some of the other recipes, and taste delightful just as they are.

300 g/10 oz buckwheat, sprouted
  (see page 18)
2 tbsp flaxseed, ground
1 lemon
125 g/4 oz dried figs
250 ml/8 fl oz water

Makes about 15
Takes 15 minutes. You need to
sprout the buckwheat in advance,
and then dehydrate for 12 hours
You need a blender and a dehydrator

Sprout the buckwheat in advance. Grind the flaxseeds if you haven't already. Peel the lemon, remove the seeds, use all the flesh, and discard the rest. Put the lemon flesh and the remaining ingredients into the blender and puree to a smooth batter. On dehydrator sheets, make into thin cracker shapes around 8-10 cm (3-4 inches) in diameter, and dehydrate for about 10 hours. When you can, flip them, and dehydrate on the other side for another couple of hours.

Figs were one of man's first foods, and the most mentioned fruit in the Bible. They contain more fibre than any other fruit or vegetable.

BANANA DATE COOKIES

These cookies were inspired by Jo's Cake (page 157).
The cake is so popular, I thought I would see if a raw version is as delectable – it is!

200 g/6½ oz rolled oats, soaked
  2-4 hours
2 tbsp flaxseed, ground
3 bananas
125 ml/4 fl oz extra virgin olive oil
180 g/6 oz fresh dates
1 tsp cinnamon

Makes about 25
Takes 15 minutes, and you need to
pre-soak your oats for 2-4 hours.
Dehydrating time is 18 hours
You need a food processor or high
power blender, plus a dehydrator

Pre-soak the oats. Grind your flaxseeds if you haven't already. Mash the bananas in the food processor or high power blender until there are no lumps left. Blend the extra virgin olive oil, bananas, oats and dates in the blender until the oats are completely broken down, and the mixture is a smooth batter. Finally, add in the cinnamon and flaxseeds and process again, until you have a thick gloopy mass. Place dessertspoons of the mixture onto the dehydrating sheet and dehydrate for 12 hours. Flip and dry on the other side for another 6 hours. Store in the fridge, they will keep for up to a week.

Bananas are the most popular fruit in the world. They contain elements of almost all we need nutritionally, including all eight of the essential amino acids.

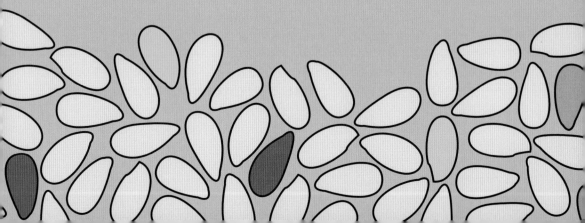

COCONUT COOKIES

These are divine! Fresh coconut is so good for you, and a vital source of saturated fats. You could use dried coconut if you don't have fresh, but it's not nearly as nice.

4 bananas
200 g/6½ oz fresh brown
  coconut
125 g/4 oz cashews, ground
125 g/4 oz raisins

Makes about 20 // Takes 15 minutes with 18 hours dehydrating // You need a food processor and dehydrator

Prepare the bananas and coconut for your food processor or high power blender. Grind the cashews if you haven't already. Put the bananas in a food processor, and process until liquefied. Add the coconut chunks, and mix until it is finely chopped. You want it left in pieces the size of rice grains, so it still has a nice chewy texture. Then add the cashews, and process briefly until they are evenly mixed in. Lastly, stir in the raisins with a spoon. Put dollops of the mixture onto dehydrator trays, and dehydrate for around 12 hours. Flip, and dry another 6 hours on the other side.

VARIATIONS:

Replace banana with 250 g/8 oz apple and 1 tbsp vanilla powder. Dehydrate 12 hours only.

FLAPJACKS

A firm favourite in our family, and unbelievably similar to the cooked version.
If I had known how to make things like this when I first got interested in raw foods,
it would have made the transition a lot easier.

250 g/8 oz rolled oats, soaked 2-4
  hours
125 ml/4 fl oz extra virgin olive oil
125 ml/4 fl oz agave syrup
2 tsp cinnamon
60 g/2 oz raisins
60 g/2 oz apple, chopped finely

Makes 18 // Takes 15 minutes, with 2-4 hours pre-soaking, and 12-18 hours dehydrating time // You need a food processor or a high power blender, and ideally a dehydrator

Put the oats in the food processor or high power blender, process for a few minutes, making sure that the grains are completely broken down into a paste. Add the extra virgin olive oil, agave, and cinnamon, and process to a smooth batter. Lastly, stir in the raisins and apple with a spoon. Spread into a square about 1 cm/½ inch high on a dehydrator sheet. Dehydrate for about 12 hours. Cut into fingers (six up by three down), then flip and dry on the other side for about 6 hours. This is one that works okay in the oven if you haven't got a dehydrator. Cooking times will depend on your oven.

Apple and raisin flapjacks are my favourite, but you can substitute whatever nut or fruit you like, or add 2 tbsp carob powder for a carob flapjack.

Raw food preparation is marvellous for children to participate in. Most recipes have very simple methods that children can be fully involved in; what's more, they can taste the fruits of their labours immediately, with no need to worry about indigestion if they eat too much of the mixture!

Cacao powder is the raw chocolate solids that haven't been roasted. Conventional cocoa powder is always roasted, so losing a lot of its nutrients and health benefits. Cocoa powder will do as a substitute, but cacao powder is now widely available in health food stores across the UK.

CHOCOLATE FLAPJACKS

Who can resist a chocolate flapjack?
And when they are this good for you, why would you want to?

250 g/8 oz rolled oats, soaked
   2-4 hours
90 g/3 oz cacao powder
6 tbsp agave syrup
6 tbsp extra virgin olive oil
6 tbsp water
60 g/2 oz raw chocolate bar
60 g/2 oz dried white
   mulberries

Pre-soak the oats for 2-4 hours. Drain and then put in the high power blender or food processor with the cacao, agave, olive oil and water. Blend to a thick puree. Chop your raw chocolate bar into tiny chunks and stir it into the mixture with the mulberries. Spread into a square on your dehydrator tray, about 1 cm/½ inch thick. Dry for 12 hours and then score into 25 squares (five across by five down). Flip, and dry for another 6 hours on the other side. If you haven't got a dehydrator, try it in your oven on the lowest temperature. Cooking times will vary according to your oven. Store in an airtight container in the fridge, and eat within a couple of weeks.

Makes 25
Takes 15 minutes with 2-5 hours pre-soaking, and 12-18 hours dehydrating time
You need a food processor or high power blender, and ideally a dehydrator, although an oven will do

Sweet Things

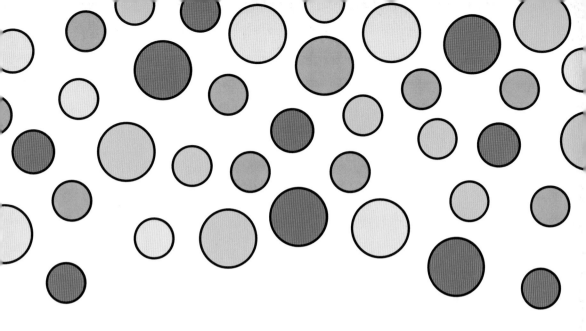

When I make sweets, I use measuring cups to make life easy. The basic recipe is 2 cups dried fruit to 1 cup nuts or seeds. They are best made in a high power blender or food grinder, but if you don't have one a food processor will do fine. Use dried dates, unless otherwise stated.

They are so popular, especially with children. It is such an easy way to introduce healthy snacks, and incredibly simple to make. You can use whatever combination of nuts and dried fruits that you choose; listed here are some of my favourites. Decorated with sesame seeds or grated coconut, they make lovely homemade gifts. If you're a chocolate fan, you can melt chocolate and dip the balls in them for chocolate coated candies. I make my own raw chocolate and dip them in that. Each recipe makes about 25 sweets.

METHOD

Grind the nuts or seeds, either in a food grinder or high power blender. Remove them and put them in a bowl or a food processor. Grind the dried fruit and add that to your bowl or food processor. Add any extra ingredients in with your mixture. If you're doing it by hand, mix together firmly with a wooden spoon. If you're doing it in the food processor, process until it becomes one solid mass; this will take a few minutes, be patient. With either method, it may be that you need to add a few drops of water or a splash of agave to hold it all together – be careful though, because too much and it will go all soggy. Once it's become a single solid mass, take walnut-sized balls of the mixture and roll between the palms of your hands to form balls. Store in the fridge.

APRICOT ENERGY BALLS

Both apricots and raisins are high in iron, which is especially important for women.

150 g/5 oz walnuts
125 g/4 oz dried apricots

125 g/4 oz raisins
1 tsp cinnamon powder

COCONUT KISSES

Fresh dates and coconut go really well together and make a charming snack just as they are.

100 g/3 ½ oz fresh brown coconut
125 g/4 oz fresh dates

125 g/4 oz raisins
1 tbsp cacao powder

HALVA

When I make these, I find it really hard not to eat them all as I make them. If I want to have any left after the family has got to them, I have to triple or quadruple the recipe

250 g/8 oz tahini
125 g/4 oz raisins

125 g/4 oz dates
1 tbsp vanilla powder

WHITE 'CHOCOLATE'

Although they may not look anything like their namesake,
they have a similarly luxurious creamy taste.

250 g/8 oz cashews
125 g/4 oz dates

125 g/4 oz raisins

CALCIUM CANDIES

Both almonds and figs are very high in calcium, so these are especially suitable to give to children.

125 g/4 oz almonds
250 g/8 oz dried figs

1 tbsp lemon juice

Picture opposite: front, white 'chocolate', coconut ice, apricot energy balls

SELENIUM SWEETS

Brazil nuts are the highest natural source of selenium. Good for the boys!

125 g/4 oz brazil nuts
125 g/4 oz raisins

125 g/4 oz dates or dried apricots
1 tbsp cacao powder

MACA BLISS BALLS

Maca is one of my favourite superfoods, I eat it most days.
Here's an easy way to get it in you that everyone loves.

125 g/4 oz tahini
125 g/4 oz raisins

1 tbsp maca

CHRISTMAS SWEETS

Like miniature Christmas puddings.

125 g/4 oz almonds
125 g/4 oz dried figs
125 g/4 oz raisins
1 tsp cinnamon
juice ½ orange
pinch ground cloves
pinch grated nutmeg

Makes about 25 sweets // Takes 15 minutes
You need either a food processor and a grinder,
or a high power blender

Almonds are the only alkaline nuts, all other nuts are acidic, so
they are the ones I like to use best. Coconut is the easiest nut
for the body to digest; all other nuts are quite taxing for the liver.

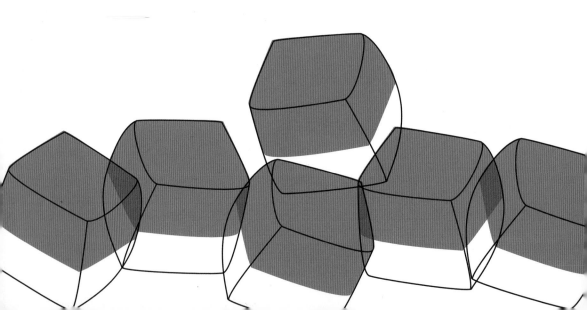

COCONUT ICE

A very popular sweet. If you're feeling lazy, miss out the beetroot and make a plain white sweet. If you can't get fresh beetroot juice, best to omit it rather than use artificial colouring. Beetroot juice has a sweet taste so it won't affect the flavour of your candy adversely.

400 g/13 oz creamed coconut
250 g/8 oz dates
1 beetroot, peeled and juiced
2 tbsp grated coconut

You can use the blocks of creamed coconut you find in Asian stores, although these are not raw. As coconut is a saturated fat it is more heat-stable, so it's not so vital that we eat it raw, unlike most other fats. If you prefer your recipe to be fully raw, you can use the flesh of a coconut to make your own by following the instructions for nut butter on page 38. Or you can buy something called coconut butter from the USA and the continent which is the same as creamed coconut: this is the whole flesh, pressed. Coconut oil is the fat removed (although confusingly, many companies in the UK sell coconut oil and label it coconut butter, as it comes to us in solid rather than liquid form). However you choose to purchase it, either leave it in a warm place to melt, or break it into chunks, and put it in the food processor, processing until it turns into a runny mass with no lumps. Break down the dates in the food processor separately, until they form a homogenized mass. Then mix the dates and coconut together in the food processor until you get a smooth paste.

Makes about 45 squares
Takes 20 minutes
You need a food processor or high power blender

Divide the mixture into two halves. Add the beetroot juice to one half of the mixture a few drops at a time, until it is a nice pink colour. Press the white half into a 23 cm (9 inch) lined tray or silicon mould, and then press the pink half on top. Sprinkle grated coconut evenly over the top, and press in. Leave to set in the fridge for a few hours. When it is hard chop into squares.

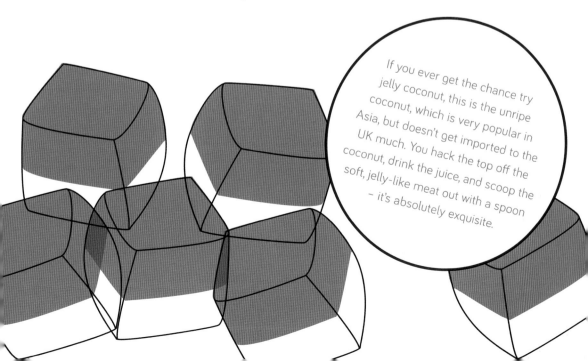

If you ever get the chance try jelly coconut, this is the unripe coconut, which is very popular in Asia, but doesn't get imported to the UK much. You hack the top off the coconut, drink the juice, and scoop the soft, jelly-like meat out with a spoon – it's absolutely exquisite.

RAW FRUIT AND NUT CHOCOLATE

When I wrote the first edition of this book, we didn't know what raw chocolate was. It was American raw food pioneer David Wolfe who popularized its usage, and our company was one of the first to sell raw chocolate in Europe, back in 2005. I think we were actually the first people in the world to make raw chocolate bars. Now raw chocolate is almost more well known than the raw food diet itself. People are understandably attracted to the idea of something that tastes so luxurious and decadent and yet is so superhealthy and good for you. Here's a basic recipe to get you started. Have fun!

100 g/3 oz coconut oil
100 g/3 oz cacao nibs
100 g/3 oz carob powder
1 tbsp agave syrup
1 tbsp vanilla powder
50 g/1½ oz raisins
50 g/1½ oz chopped nuts
  e.g. brazils, cashews, hazelnuts

Makes about 40 squares
Takes 15 minutes,
with up to 2 hours setting time
You need a grinder or high power
blender

Melt the coconut oil in a heat-proof bowl stood in a pan of simmering water, or a porringer or a Thermomix. Grind the nibs in your grinder or high power blender. Add the carob to the high power blender or transfer to a food processor (I prefer Peruvian carob to Mediterranean, it is sweeter and more caramelly). Add the agave, vanilla, and coconut oil and process again until smooth. Stir in the raisins and nuts by hand. When your chocolate is ready it should be a thick pouring consistency. Pour into silicon moulds, or line a tray with greaseproof paper, silver foil or cling film. If you're in a hurry, you can put it in the freezer to set – in silicon moulds it just takes 10 minutes. Otherwise, put it in the fridge – it will take 2 hours in a normal tray or 30 minutes in silicon moulds. Keeps well stored in the fridge in an airtight container for up to a month.

Cacao in its pure form is a powerhouse of nutrients including magnesium, sulphur, iron and antioxidants. Chocolate has a bad reputation, but it's the hydrogenated fats, refined sugars, and processed dairy products that go into conventional chocolate bars that are a problem, not the actual cacao bean itself.

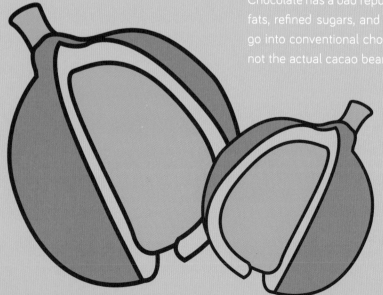

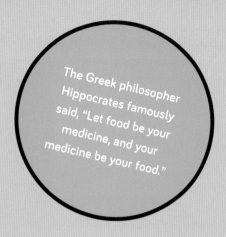

The Greek philosopher Hippocrates famously said, "Let food be your medicine, and your medicine be your food."

CASHEW CREAM

The cashews you buy in supermarkets and health food stores are never raw. Look for hand-cracked cashews which are far superior in flavour and texture.

125 g/4 oz cashews, soaked 4-8 hours
60 g/2 oz dates
1 tbsp vanilla powder
2 tbsp olive oil
water

Pre-soak the cashews. Blend all the ingredients. Start off with half a cup of water (125 ml/4 fl oz) and then add a tablespoon at a time until you reach the desired consistency. Half a cup makes a thick cream, one cup (250 ml/8 fl oz) for a runny pouring cream.

This is marvellous with any pudding, such as fruit salad (page 105) or Apple Crumble (page 114), or you can use it as icing for a cake.

Serves 8-12 // Takes 10 minutes, with 4-8 hours pre-soaking for cashews // You need a blender

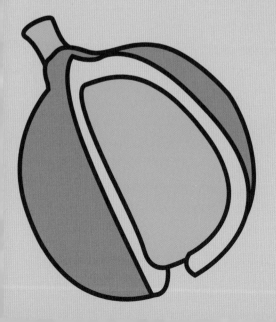

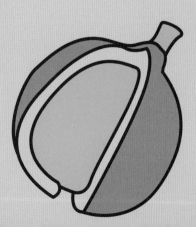

TOFFEE SPREAD

This makes an incredibly thick, sticky spread, very intense in flavour and rammed with nutrients. Spread sparingly on crackers or Essene bread.

125 g/4 oz yacon syrup or raw honey
60 g/2 oz flaxseed, ground
1 tbsp cacao powder
1 tsp vanilla powder

Make sure you've got your ground flaxseeds ready. With a wooden spoon, combine the yacon syrup and flaxseed, then add the cacao and vanilla. Keeps indefinitely.

Makes 20 servings // Take 5 minutes
You need a grinder

CHOCOLATE SAUCE

Pour over chopped fruit, or have a raw fondue and dip slices of fruit into the carob sauce.

1 banana
2 tbsp cacao powder
1 tbsp agave syrup or raw honey
1 tbsp tahini
water

Makes 8 servings
Takes 5 minutes
You need a blender

Break the banana into chunks and put all the ingredients in the blender. Blend until you get a smooth creamy sauce. Add water according to how thick you want the sauce: a little for a fruit dip, more for a fruit dressing.

If you don't like chocolate, you can use carob powder instead. Carob powder is made from the pods of the fruit, not the seeds. If you are lucky enough to find carob pods they make wonderful snacks: you chew on the pod and spit out the seeds.

CHOCOLATE SPREAD

This goes wonderfully on crackers and loaves.

2 bananas
60 g/2 oz almond butter
2 tbsp cacao powder
1 tbsp maca (optional)

Serves 8
Takes 10 minutes
You need a blender

Break down the bananas in the food processor until they are liquefied. Add the almond butter, then cacao powder, and maca if you're using it, process to a thick paste. If it's not sweet enough for your tastes, add a little agave or raw honey.

Cacao is chocolate powder that hasn't been roasted. The caffeine in raw chocolate is thought to be inactive, so if you are sensitive to caffeine, like I am, you should be ok with raw chocolate.

Drinks

REJUVELAC WINE

JUICES

CARROT AND APPLE

CARROT AND ORANGE

BEETROOT

APPLE AND GINGER

CUCUMBER AND MINT

ORANGE AND APPLE

GREEN JUICE

PEACH

SUNSHINE JUICE

SMOOTHIES

SUPER SMOOTHIE

GUAVA 1.0

HEAVEN IN A GLASS

CREAMY GUAVA

CAROB SHAKE

MILKS

ALMOND MILK

BANANA MILK

REJUVELAC WINE

Rejuvelac is the name given to the soak water of wheat grain. It is full of nutrients and enzymes. Anne Wigmore, who founded the Hippocrates Health Institute was a great believer in the restorative powers of fermented foods such as rejuvelac and sauerkraut.

2 tbsp wheat grain
2 tbsp dried fruit
1 tbsp seeds or nuts
½ cinnamon stick
1 cm/½ inch piece fresh ginger
3 fresh cloves

Place all the ingredients in a large jar, and fill with about 650 ml /1 ¼ pint pure water. Leave for 12 hours. At the end of this time, place the contents of the jar in the blender and blend until completely liquefied. Then transfer back to the jar, and leave for a further 24 hours. Finally, strain and serve.

Next time you soak wheat for sprouting, don't throw the water away. You can drink it neat, or if the taste is too much for you, mix it with other drinks. Many raw foodists use rejuvelac in place of pure water in recipes such as soups and pâtés. If you mix rejuvelac with ground seeds, and leave it to ferment for a day or two, it makes a seed cheese which you can use as an accompaniment to salads or as a spread for crackers.

Serves 3
Takes 5 minutes, with 36 hours fermenting time
You need a blender

JUICES

Juices are the best way to get a blast of nutrients without taxing your digestive system. Freshly made juice is incomparable to the shop-bought version, and once you've started making your own, you won't ever want to go back to the packaged stuff. Orange juice, for instance, loses 70 % of its nutritional value within an hour of it being squeezed. There are many quality books on the market about the benefits of juicing and suggestions for recipes. I've just included here a few of my favourites, but the permutations are endless. Just one rule: for ease of digestion, don't mix fruits and vegetables, carrots and apples being the only exceptions. Apples work particularly well in adding sweetness to some of the more bitter vegetable juices.

Remove any unwanted stems, roots etc. Peel oranges and beetroot. Feed all ingredients through the juicer and drink immediately. For best results, if you're using lemon, or any herbs and spices, juice them in the middle of the other ingredients, not first or last, to make sure they get properly juiced.

I don't actually own a juicer, although I drink a lot of juice. My preferred method of juicing is to put all the ingredients in a blender and then strain through a milk bag. It's much quicker and easier, very efficient, and there's no washing the juicer afterwards!

Each recipe makes 200-300 ml (around ½ pint)

CARROT AND APPLE

Very good for the digestion.

3 carrots

1 apple

1 stick celery

¼ red chilli pepper (optional)

BEETROOT

Beetroot is a good liver cleanser. Great for a hangover!

3 small beetroot

1 apple

CUCUMBER AND MINT

Very refreshing on a summer's day. Cucumbers are the most cooling vegetables.

1 cucumber

1 apple

1 sprig mint

GREEN JUICE

Drinking green juice every day is one of the best things you can do for your health.

1 cucumber

½ head celery

1 lemon (all the flesh, peel removed)

1 clove garlic

2 handfuls greens e.g. spinach, parsley, kale

SUNSHINE JUICE

Markets often sell big bags of peppers for next to nothing, and this is a lovely way to use them up.

1 red pepper

1 yellow pepper

1 apple

CARROT AND ORANGE
Blend in an avocado, and you've got a soup!

3 carrots   2 oranges

APPLE AND GINGER
Experiment with different varieties of apple, you'll be amazed at the difference in flavour.

3 apples   1 cm/½ inch piece fresh ginger
¼ lemon (unwaxed, with peel on)

ORANGE AND APPLE
I used to love to have this for breakfast, usually with a good dose of ginger, some Klamath
Lake blue-green algae, and a teaspoon of flax oil all stirred in.

2 apples   ¼ lemon (unwaxed, with peel on)
2 oranges

PEACH
Juicing the lemon peel as well adds an extra zest to your juice.

2 apples   ¼ lemon (unwaxed, with peel on)
1 peach

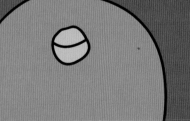

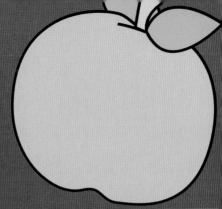

SMOOTHIES

Smoothies have become a staple item in the past decade and now you can find them in every supermarket and corner shop. Although there are some fine makes around, they are likely to have been pasteurised so they are not raw. You can't beat doing it yourself, and it's so quick and easy. A meal in the glass, they serve well as breakfast or lunch when you're in a hurry, or make an easily digested dessert.

Each recipe makes 200-300 ml (around ½ pint)

SUPER SMOOTHIE

3 pieces of fruit, juiced
½ banana (frozen for a thicker smoothie)

1 piece fresh fruit
1 tsp lecithin granules

Put all the ingredients in the blender and puree until smooth. For an extra energy lift, add some Aloe vera, maca, or Kl0amath Lake blue-green algae. For a beneficial dose of essential fatty acids, add 1-2 tsp flax oil.

HEAVEN IN A GLASS
This is my all-time favourite smoothie.

1 medium mango
3 oranges, juiced
¼ lemon (unwaxed, with peel on)

1 tsp tahini
1 date
½ frozen banana

CAROB SHAKE

There are many different makes of grain coffee on the market, all much the same: a blend of barley, rye, chicory, and figs, which tastes not dissimilar to coffee. I often add a little when I am using carob in a recipe to deepen the flavour and give it more of a dark chocolate taste.

3 apples, juiced
2 tbsp dates
1 tbsp tahini
1 tbsp carob powder
1 tsp cinnamon
1 tsp grain coffee

GUAVA 1.0

Guavas are overall one of the most nutritious fruits on the planet. They bring a wonderful tropical aroma to my kitchen, and add an exotic touch to any smoothie.

3 apples, juiced
1 guava
½ banana
¼ lemon (unwaxed, with peel on)

CREAMY GUAVA

Guavas are a wonderful source of vitamin C, vitamin B1, vitamin B2, niacin and phosphorus.

2 pears, juiced
1 apple, juiced
1 guava
2 tbsp soya or goat's yoghurt
¼ lemon (unwaxed, with peel on)

MILKS

There are many different alternatives to cow's milk in the shops now, such as rice milk, oat milk, and of course soya milk. If you can find raw goat's milk or sheep's milk, many raw fooders choose to include that in their diets, as a good source of vitamin D. Which milk you pick depends on your body's individual needs and your own personal taste preference. However, I would recommend making your own nut and seed milks as the best choice. It takes no time at all, it's very cheap, and just as delicious. They must be consumed fresh however – milks don't usually last much beyond 12 hours, so only make as much as you need in a day.

ALMOND MILK

2 tbsp almonds, soaked 2-4 hours
600 ml/1 pint water

Blend for a minute. Strain and serve. Add sweetener if desired e.g. date, banana, apple. I like to use a milk bag for straining. They are handy and inexpensive pieces of equipment to have in the kitchen. If you don't have one, you can just strain through a sieve.

BANANA MILK

1 banana
250 ml/8 fl oz water

Blend for a few minutes until the banana is liquefied.

You can make milk with virtually any nut, seed or vegetable when you blend it with water, but these are two of the tastiest and most nutritious options. Sesame milk is also popular, but a little bitter. I use shelled hemp seeds a lot because they don't need straining.

Not
Really Raw

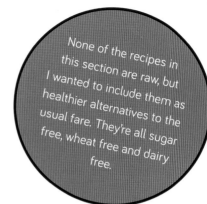

None of the recipes in this section are raw, but I wanted to include them as healthier alternatives to the usual fare. They're all sugar free, wheat free and dairy free.

I always advise people to aim low when transitioning to raw foods. Better to be 50% raw, feel the benefits, and feel enthused to do more, than push yourself to be 100% raw, feel like you are missing out on all your favourite cooked foods, and then give up because it's too hard. It's all a question of learning to listen to and trust your body, and have faith in the body's wisdom.

If you're including cooked foods in your diet, there are some that are better to include than others. The healthiest cooked foods I would recommend eating are firstly cooked vegetables, and then quinoa and millet. You may find you can satisfy your cooked cravings just with these foods alone. Here are a few of my favourite cooked recipes from when I was transitioning to 100% raw.

PERFECT POTATO SALAD

As potatoes raise the blood sugar level, it's not sensible to eat them in large quantities.
And unfortunately this staple part of the British diet isn't particularly edible raw.
So whenever you serve them it's a good idea to substitute sweet potatoes
for at least half the quantity of white potatoes.

180 g/6 oz white potatoes
180 g/6 oz sweet potatoes
1 tbsp hemp seeds
2 tbsp chopped spring onion
1 tbsp fresh parsley, finely chopped
2 tbsp mayonnaise
salt and pepper, to taste

Chop both types of potato, into cubes about 2.5 cm (1 inch) square. Bring to the boil, and simmer for 8 minutes. Leave to cool, then transfer to a bowl, and with a spoon, toss with the remaining ingredients.

Serves 2 // Takes 20 minutes
You don't need any special equipment

CHAMPION CHIPS

It was years before I stopped craving chips. This is what I would have, and it is a relatively healthy option, as well as being far yummier than any oven or chip shop chip.

180 g/6 oz potatoes
180 g/6 oz sweet potatoes
1 tbsp extra virgin olive oil or
   coconut oil
1 tbsp tamari

Serves 2
Takes 10 minutes with 15 minutes
cooking time
You don't need any special
equipment

Chop potatoes into fingers about 10 x 1.5 cm (4 x ½ inch). Place on a baking tray and pour over just enough oil and tamari to coat them. Bake 200°C/425°F/gas mark 7 for 15 minutes. Take the chips out and stir them, if necessary adding some more extra virgin olive oil to prevent sticking. Cook for a further fifteen minutes. Serve with a large green salad.

Other vegetables that make delectable chips are celeriac, beetroot, and squash. Parsnips are good, but you need to steam or blanch them for a few minutes first or they will be too woody.

REUBEN'S STEW

This is the favourite dinner of my eldest son, Reuben, right now. If you want to keep it raw, you can just heat it at a low temperature. Otherwise, cooking times are very short to preserve the nutritional value of the vegetables.

4 tomatoes
handful fresh basil
1 tsp tamari
1 tbsp vegetable bouillon
1.5 litres/3 pints water
60 g/2 oz green beans
2 carrots
1 small head broccoli
4 mushrooms
60 g/2 oz cauliflower
½ red onion
4 cloves garlic

Prepare all your vegetables for the saucepan. Boil the water in the kettle. We make this in the Thermomix, that way you can heat it and be sure it's not cooking. Blend together the tomatoes, basil, tamari, bouillon and water to make a sauce. Pour that into your pan. Dice your vegetables and add them into the sauce. Simmer as long as you like, until the vegetables are tender enough for your taste. Serve immediately.

Serves 2
Takes 10 minutes to prepare, cooking time is up to you
You need a blender

NANA'S CHUTNEY

This chutney is easy to make, and goes well with just about any salad. Much better than a shop-bought jar full of sugar and salt.

180 ml/6 fl oz apple cider vinegar
3 tbsp yacon syrup or raw honey
125 g/4 oz dates, chopped
2 cloves garlic, finely chopped
0.5 cm/¼ inch piece fresh ginger, finely chopped
½ red chilli pepper, finely chopped
2 tbsp raisins
1 tsp miso

Put vinegar and molasses in a pan and bring to the boil. Add dates, garlic, chilli and ginger, and simmer gently for 15 minutes, stirring occasionally to prevent sticking. Next, add the raisins and simmer for a further 5 minutes, stirring occasionally. Stir in the miso at the end of cooking. Leave to cool and transfer to a jar. Store in the fridge; keeps indefinitely.

This is adapted from a recipe my grandmother gave me. Although it is cooked, it has so many of my favourite ingredients in I couldn't leave it out.

Makes 8 servings // Takes 30 minutes // You don't need any special equipment

JO'S CAKE

This is the best cake ever – no nasties, and still so scrumptious. It's the only really stunning wheat-free, sugar-free, dairy-free cake I've ever come across.

60 g/2 oz rolled oats
125 ml/4 fl oz extra virgin olive oil
180 g/6 oz dates
3 bananas
90 g/3 oz soya flour
90 g/3 oz rice flour
3 tsp bicarbonate of soda

ICING
300 g/10 oz tahini
6 tbsp agave syrup
30 g/1 oz carob or cacao powder
water

Serves 8 // Takes 15 minutes with 1 hour baking time, plus additional time to make the frosting // You need a food processor

Break the oats down into flour in a food processor, remove and set aside. Break down the dates in a food processor until they form a homogenized mass. Then add bananas, extra virgin olive oil, and oats to the dates, and process again to make a smooth batter. Put in the rest of the ingredients and process once more until they are completely mixed in. Spoon into a greased 19 cm (7½ inch) cake tin and bake 160°C/325°F/gas mark 3 for 60-70 minutes. Turn out, and ice when cool.

To make the icing, put all the ingredients in a bowl, and stir together with a spoon, adding a little water at a time until it is the right consistency – thin enough to spread, but not too runny.

Jo gave me this recipe when our children were toddlers and best friends, and I have used it ever since whenever a birthday cake is called for. It has a gorgeous, light taste, is quick and easy to make, and someone always asks for the recipe.

Afterword

RAW LIVING

Founded in 2002, at the same time as the original publication of this book, my website Raw Living is now Europe's biggest online raw foods and superfoods store, with the widest selection of gourmet raw food snacks, staples and superfoods that you will find outside of the USA. There are also lots of articles, recipes and useful information on the site for you to browse.

If there are any ingredients that you've read about here which are unfamiliar or you're not sure where to find them, be assured that we stock them all!

http://rawliving.eu   01243 523335

KATE'S MAGIC BUBBLE

This is my members' site full of inspiration and motivation. Every week I post new recipes, articles, interviews and videos. Joining the Bubble is the best way to be kept up to date with all my latest work. Members also get discounts on their Raw Living shopping, and can ask me questions through the site.

http://katesmagicbubble.com

RAW MAGIC EVENTS AND COURSES

I have a very busy international schedule, lecturing, teaching workshops and leading courses mostly in Europe but also around the world. I do one day food prep classes, and also five day Raw Magic advanced courses for the full low down. Check out the events pages on Raw Living and the Bubble for all the information and my upcoming tour dates.

KATE MAGIC BOOKS

Raw Living is my second book. It was published by Grub Street in 2007. It is full of quick and easy recipes like this book, although it helps if you have a bit of raw food knowledge already, and are the proud owner of a high power blender and dehydrator.

Raw Magic is my third book. It was published by Process Media in 2012. Although all the recipes are raw, it is primarily a superfoods recipe book. It's full of information about superfoods, their benefits, and how to use them. All the recipes are crammed full of superfoods.

These are some of the people who inspire me in the kitchen.
Find their websites, read their books, eat their food....

Solla (Iceland), Annie Jubb (USA), Ani Phyo (USA), Caroline Fibaek (Denmark), Julia Corbett (USA), Natalia KW (USA), Anna Middleton (UK), Alex Malinsky (USA), David Wolfe (USA), Gabriel Cousens (USA), Boris Lauser (Berlin).

Index